Date Due

Hensall			

133114

971   Daniells, R.
.201   Alexander Mackenzie
0924   and the North West.
Macke

350

133114

971   Daniells, Roy.
.201   Alexander Mackenzie and the North West.
0924   Toronto, Oxford University Press, 1971.
Macke   219 p. illus., maps. (Canadian lives)
          Includes bibliography.

RELATED }   1. Mackenzie, Sir Alexander, 1763–1820.
BOOKS IN }   2. Northwest, Canadian – Discovery and
CATALOG }   exploration. I. Title.
UNDER   }
                                     G–6905

                                     G 6225

Sir Alexander Mackenzie by Sir Thomas Lawrence
The National Gallery of Canada, Ottawa
Canadian War Memorials Collection

ALEXANDER MACKENZIE
and the North West

Roy Daniells

'It is no mere accident that the present
Dominion coincides roughly with the fur-
trading areas of northern North America.'

H. A. INNIS

Toronto

OXFORD UNIVERSITY PRESS

1971

First published in 1969 by Faber and Faber Limited.
First published in this paperback edition in 1971.

ISBN 0-19-540186-7

© Roy Daniells

2 3 4 5 — 5 4 3 2

Printed in Canada

Preface

MY indebtedness to the expertise of friends exceeds any acknowledgement possible within the restrictions of a preface but gratitude is not the less real for being briefly indicated. Dr Kaye Lamb, whose forthcoming book under the Hakluyt Society imprint will include Mackenzie's letters; Professor Victor Hopwood, whose special interest is in the explorer David Thompson; Professors J. R. Mackay and J. K. Stager, who have an intimate knowledge of northern terrain; the Librarian of the University of British Columbia, Basil Stuart-Stubbs, and Professor C. Verner, who furnished and interpreted maps; Mr Donald Bruce, who produced pictures of the Peace River; Dr George Woodcock, the editor of the series, who suggested many essential revisions of and additions to the text; Mr Malcolm Nicolson and Mr Ian Morrison of the Nicolson Institute in Stornoway, who recaptured Mackenzie's boyhood; the staff of the Library of the University of British Columbia: to each and all, my thanks.

For illustrations I am indebted to the Public Archives of Canada, the National Gallery of Canada, the Government of British Columbia (Department of Travel), and especially to Professor J. R. Mackay. The quotation on the title-page is from *The Fur Trade in Canada* (University of Toronto Press and Yale University Press). The Public Archives of Canada has given permission for quotation as follows: p. 29, ll. 11–27 (*Hardwicke Papers*, 35, 915, Pt. I, pp. 165–6); p. 55, ll. 25–30 (C11A, LXXXIII, 161); p. 189, ll. 18–26 (*Selkirk Papers*, II, 167); p. 189, l. 30; p. 190, l. 6 (Q, CXX, 90); p. 191, ll. 15–22 (*Minutes of the Northwest Company*, p. 43).

7

Contents

Illustrations

Introduction

The Country of the Birch-bark Canoe

BENEATH the lion and the unicorn supporting the coat of arms of the Dominion of Canada the legend reads A MARI USQUE AD MARE. It is taken from a Biblical text, 'He shall have dominion also from sea to sea and from the river to the ends of the earth.' The Canadian reinterprets this verse of an old Hebrew psalm and gives it a meaning adapted to the geography of Canada—from Atlantic Ocean to Pacific and from the St Lawrence River to the remote Arctic regions.

These words are also an exact description of the explorations carried through by Alexander Mackenzie, the eighteenth-century Scottish fur trader who is the subject of this book. From Montreal, on the bank of the St Lawrence, he moved into the land of the great northern lakes and from there, in 1789, he first penetrated to the Arctic, then, by another voyage, four years later, pierced the Rocky Mountains to reach Bella Coola on the Pacific coast.

Unlike travellers who reach the courts of eastern emperors, or navigators who quell mutinies and land on hostile shores, or explorers who find the ruins of great civilizations, Mackenzie tells of voyages that are strangely unspectacular. He never fired on an Indian; he never lied or deceived; he never lost a man of his party. Yet he was constantly in danger and amid hardships; his material resources were very slender; he was operating from a base thousands of miles distant from the settled parts of Canada. Watching him on one of his

13

carefully timed journeys, filled with hairsbreadth chances and studded with menacing obstacles, is to become convinced that imagination, courage and power of will can be effective in the affairs of men and that decisive turning points in the history of a country are often reached without excitement or fanfare.

As we follow Mackenzie's explorations, we shall have to keep beside us, or in our mind's eye, three maps. The first is a map of the world as an eighteenth-century British merchant would conceive it. Centres of trade like London, New York, Canton or Montreal are main points of reference. Ocean routes, to the far East or to the Americas, are linked to the island of Great Britain. Spheres of influence within which dominant nations, like Spain, or powerful corporations, like the East India Company, operate must be marked out, though their boundaries often change.

A second map is that of western Canada, as we should now call it, that is, everything west of the Great Lakes and north of the 49th parallel. As we begin our story, much of this enormous territory is unknown. When we conclude, it will be, in its essentials, firmly delineated on our developing map.

A third map is that showing, on a larger scale and in more detail, the actual routes taken by Mackenzie, first to the Arctic, then to the Pacific. His base is Lake Athabasca.

As we consider the last two maps—and we shall be doing so continually—we must keep in mind the enormous area they depict. The drainage basin of the Mackenzie River is rather less than 500,000 square miles. The area of Canada is about 3,845,000 square miles. To achieve a rough but useful sense of Canada's geographical situation, we might think of the world as an orange. Two cuts in the rind (along the 50th and 140th west meridians), meeting on the North Pole

Beach on Mackenzie River

J. R. Mackay

Pavement of boulders shoved by ice: bank of Mackenzie River

J. R. Mackay

at right angles, and a third cut traversing them halfway between pole and equator will enable us to peel off a triangular surface corresponding to the area within which Canada's history has taken place, including once hopeful claims to the valley of the Columbia River, disputed fishing rights off Newfoundland, and a great wedge of permanent polar ice. To follow Mackenzie's travels within this area and to feel with him in his concern for logistics is to learn a good deal about Canada. He had to move heavy loads of trade goods and supplies over long distances, with limited manpower, and he had to bring out furs, bargained for, not plundered, to pay for this expenditure of effort and, if possible, to show a profit. This is what Canadians are still trying to do. They are still peering at maps with Mackenzie's kind of anxiety, calculation and hope, though now they are concerned with coal and ore, with oil and wheat and potash.

As well as pausing to look at maps, we shall have to follow Mackenzie's thoughts on such diverse matters as the building of bark canoes, the organization of the fur trade and the use of instruments of navigation. He considered such things very carefully, so that when the time came to act he was fully prepared and sure of his plans. He was not well educated but he was a clear thinker with an extraordinary capacity to translate thought into action.

The thing uppermost in his mind was transport by water. In the absence of roads, the only practicable method of moving trade goods, furs and men was along navigable streams and lakes to eastern ports accessible to ships which had crossed the Atlantic. Mackenzie's voyages were for the purpose of establishing a similar outlet on the Pacific side. Once he had left the Great Lakes, his route was involved with streams and lakes, many of which are today still very

THE EXPLORATIONS
OF
ALEXANDER MACKENZIE

```
••••••••••••  FUR TRADERS' ROUTE FROM MONTREAL
                  TO FORT CHIPEWYAN
—·—·—·—·—  MACKENZIE'S ROUTE TO THE ARCTIC, 1789
— — — — —  MACKENZIE'S ROUTE TO THE PACIFIC, 1792-3
```

Hudson
Bay

ORT CHURCHILL

Gulf of
St. Lawrence

he Woods

Rainy
Lake

GRAND PORTAGE

Lake
Superior

MICHILIMACKINAC

Georgian
Bay

Lake
Huron

Lake
Michigan

Mississippi R.

LOWER CANADA

St. Lawrence R.

QUEBEC

MONTREAL
LACHINE

UPPER CANADA

L. Ontario

KINGSTON

NIAGARA

L. Erie

DETROIT

Atlantic
Ocean

R. H. Meyer '67

A M—B

remote and far from railways or paved roads. Even the great rivers, Peace and Mackenzie, together with Lake Athabasca and Great Slave Lake, are sights that few Canadians have seen.

To avoid confusion among the many references we shall have to make to these remote lakes and rivers, the reader should perhaps note that the Peace is formed by the confluence of the Finlay and Parsnip Rivers in the so-called Rocky Mountain Trench, just west of the main range of the Rockies, and that this takes place at 56° North Latitude, a long way north of the Columbia and Fraser. The Peace flows first east, then north until deflected by a height of land known as the Caribou Mountains, then north-east to receive the waters of Lake Claire and Lake Athabasca. It then turns due north and is called Slave River. It then flows through Great Slave Lake and as it emerges is called the Mackenzie. Its course continues, north by west, and it receives, first the waters of the Liard (itself a stream 755 miles in length), then the overflow of Great Bear Lake (which has an area of 12,000 square miles) before it reaches the Beaufort Sea, part of the Arctic Ocean.

Regardless of its three names, this is one stream. The lower reaches gave Mackenzie his road to the Arctic; the upper reaches gave him a route which would penetrate the Rocky Mountains and account for nearly two-thirds of the distance of his western journey.

The gentle reader, in the old sense of the reader courteously disposed to help the author, might also prepare himself for continuous shifts of geographical scale. At one moment, Mackenzie is hard put to it to overcome a few yards of rapid current, at another he is thinking of trans-Pacific commerce with Canton. He may be standing waist deep in a rushing river, holding on to a wrecked canoe, but this battered craft is still the needle drawing behind it a thread which, knotted with those drawn across the world's greatest oceans by Cook and Vancouver, will form the basis of a network on which Canada still depends for economic survival. Mackenzie may have been, from a military point of view, almost unarmed, yet the permanent effects of his penetration of territory were at least comparable to Marlborough's leading an army to Blenheim. As Cowper has the bard say to Boadicea:

> Regions Caesar never knew
> Thy posterity shall sway,
> Where his eagles never flew,
> None invincible as they.

The fur trade in which Mackenzie engaged had as its base the great port of Montreal. It depended on a specialized technique of transport. Whereas the Hudson's Bay Company encouraged its Indians to bring their furs to posts at tide-water on the Bay and abandoned this policy only under pressure of competition, the Montreal men were compelled from the beginning to fan out into the western prairies and forests and create new centres of trade in hitherto unknown country.

To do so, they adopted and adapted techniques which the French had already acquired from the natives. Chief among these was the use of the bark canoe.

The canoe was uniquely useful and became a symbol of exploration, because it was the only weapon with which to assault the Canadian Shield, that vast V-shaped area where hummocks of Precambrian rock stand up from muskegs drained through an immense network of lakes and rivers. Take a pencil and on any map of Canada draw a line from the Arctic shore above Great Bear Lake to the lake itself, thence through the centre of Great Slave Lake and the western tip of Lake Athabasca. Continue to the northern end of Lake Winnipeg, then from its southern end to the American border and along the border to Lake Superior. Follow the shore of the lakes to the eastern end of the Georgian Bay, then across country direct to the point where the St Lawrence flows out of Lake Ontario. Finish by running the pencil in an arc, just north of Montreal and Quebec, to meet the river again and along the north bank, which becomes the shore of the Gulf, to the Atlantic. Everything north of this line, with the exception of some Arctic islands and a wedge of lowland south of Hudson's Bay, is Shield. It covers nearly half the total area of the country. From the geologist's point of view it is an ancient and extremely complex structure inviting endless investigation. From the fur trader's viewpoint it offers a ready-made network of lakes and streams through which he has to work out a route with the fewest possible portages and the longest runs of navigable water.

The birch-bark canoe, which the white man took over from the Indian, was in no sense a localized product. The canoe birch was obtainable over most of the area of what is now Canada, though not, of course, north of the tree line and, oddly enough, not far west of the Rockies. In the far north, Eskimo had perfected the kayak, made of skins, and on the Pacific coast large softwoods were profusely available for the manufacture of dug-outs.

The birch canoe had to be very strong, to carry heavy loads and to take the strain of being steered through swift currents and boiling rapids. It had also to be extremely light, so that a few inches of water sufficed to float it and a turn of the steersman's wrist to keep it off the rocks and so that it could be portaged by one or two men up river banks and over rough ground. Its materials must be easily obtainable so that repairs could be made en route: bark, gum and split roots for sewing. The birch canoe met all these requirements and a glance at the map shows what an immense network of waterways existed on which it could be put to use. Nowhere else in the world has nature provided anything to compare with the web of lakes and rivers draining the Canadian Shield.

A French account of how canoes were made by the Indians in what is now Nova Scotia, in the seventeenth century, supplies vivid detail. From the largest birch trees they could find, the Indians removed a great sheet of bark from eighteen to twenty-seven feet long. The breadth of the canoe was about two feet in the middle. When a man sat in it, it came up to his armpits. It was lined with cedar slats, split very thin and running the whole length; these were about four inches broad and were, of course, tapered at bow and stern. The ribs were also of cedar, bent into half circles when heated. The seams were sewed with long, thin fir roots which split more easily than the osiers used in France to make baskets. Two long round sticks, as thick as a large cane, formed the gunwales and shorter sticks of beech formed thwarts. When the gunwales had been firmly sewn in and the bark shaped for bow and stern, the whole being closely lined with cedar slats, and the thwarts entered into holes in the gunwales and firmly fixed, then the hooped ribs were forcibly driven in and the canoe lined with them from one end to the other. The single sheet of bark mentioned in this early French account was, of course, generally replaced by a patchwork of pieces sewed together. The seams were payed with fir or spruce gum, chewed by the women. Melted, it was better than pitch, for its purpose. The canoe, when finished, was often light enough for a single man to carry on his head.

Details of construction, overall dimensions, and elements of design, such as height of stern and bow and the way the bark was tailored, varied from region to region. Size varied greatly; west of the Great Lakes, where trees were smaller and rainfall less, small canoes holding two or three men were popular. But the birch canoe was a unique triumph of design and construction which, like the violin, was everywhere essentially the same.

The paddle was, of course, the normal means of propelling a canoe but it could be poled in rapids by experienced hands or towed on a line. It could be sailed before a moderate wind but not manœuvred under sail, since it had no keel and the variable depth of water in the rivers made centreboard or leeboards impracticable.

A first-hand account of travel by canoe has come to us from the pen of a young officer named George Thomas Landmann, who knew Mackenzie.

'These canoes were exceedingly strong and capacious, they were about thirty-six feet in length, by six feet wide, near the middle; and although the birch bark which formed a thin external coating over the ribs of white cedar, and their longitudinal laths of the same wood, appeared to compose but a flimsy vessel, yet they usually carried a weight of five tons. It may be as well to state that this cargo was very carefully stowed, in order to remove any unequal pressure, which would have been fatal to such a vessel. Four poles, three or four inches in diameter at the thickest ends, denominated by the Canadians, *grandperch*, and nearly as long as the canoe, were laid side by side in the middle of the bottom of the canoe. On these poles, the cargo was carefully arranged so that all the weight rested on them, and none allowed to press against the bare and unprotected sides of the canoe. Every package was made up of the weight of ninety pounds and none heavier.

'The five tons included the provision for ten men, sufficient to support them during about twenty to twenty-two days. Each canoe was provided with a mast and a lug-sail, and also each man had a ten-foot setting-pole, of good ash, shod with an iron ferrule at each end, for assisting the men towing with a strong line in ascending the rapids. The paddles were supplied by the canoemen, each bringing his own. Each canoe had also a camp-kettle, provided by the owners, as also a few Hambro lines, a bundle of watap, roots of the pine-tree, for stitching up any seams that might burst, a parcel of gum of a resinous nature, for paying over the seams when leaky, a piece of birchbark for repairs, hatchet, crooked knife, and a few more indispensable articles.

'The crew consisted of a guide, a steersman, and eight common paddlers, but all worked alike. The guide was paid about as much as four ordinary men, and the steersman half as much. Sixteen to twenty pounds was about the wages of a good guide. On arriving at a carrying-place, everything was unloaded with expedition and care; and whilst six men were required to transport the canoe, the others hastened to carry the goods, each man bearing two packs, and sometimes, as a display of strength, three. The canoe I was in had twelve men, as also the other one in company, and no merchandise, nothing but provisions and our baggage, which gave us a wonderful advantage in passing the carrying-places, as two trips was always found to be sufficient to carry the whole. The carriers of the canoe had the severest work, and as it weighed about fifteen hundred pounds, it is clear that each man of the six was expected to bear, on level ground, about two hundred and fifty pounds, but under many circumstances, when the ground was at all uneven, the whole weight was unequally divided. It was very interesting to me to see the extraordinary facility with which these men reversed the canoe and in an instant shouldered it, which required great

23

expertness, as any slip or accident would have destroyed the vessel, beyond the power of repairing. . . .

'No men in the world are more severely worked than these Canadian voyageurs. I have known them to work in a canoe twenty hours out of twenty-four, and go at that rate during a fortnight or three weeks without a day of rest or a diminution of labour; but it is not with impunity they so exert themselves; they lose much flesh in the performance of such journeys, though the amount of food they consume is incredible. They smoke almost incessantly, and sing peculiar songs, which are the same their fathers and grandfathers and probably their great-grandfathers sang before them; the time is about the same as that of our military quick marches, and is marked by the movement of their paddles. They rest from five to ten minutes every two hours, when they refill their pipes; it is more common for them to describe distances by so many pipes, than in any other way.'

The North-Westers having found the birch-bark canoe the perfect conveyance and having become completely dependent upon it, they could not imagine any alternative. Alexander Ross tells how Astor's men on the Columbia made use of 'split or sawed cedar-boats, strong, light, and durable, and in every possible way safer and better adapted to rough water than the birch-rind canoes in general use on the east side of the mountains. They carried a cargo or burden of about 3000 lbs. weight, and yet, nimbly handled, were easily carried across the portages.' The North-Westers, however, were accustomed to their own birch canoes and, when they came to the Columbia, could not bring themselves to make a change. 'Therefore, the country was ransacked for prime birch bark more frequently than for prime furs; and to guard against a failure in this fanciful article, a stock of it was shipped at Montreal for London, and from thence conveyed round Cape Horn for their establishment at Fort George [Astoria], in case that none of equal quality could be found on the waters of the Pacific.' If the last statement appears beyond belief, we should remember that miners in the early Californian gold rush were not above sending their clothes to China to be washed.

In addition to the canoe, the Indian furnished the famous concentrated food known as pemmican. The name is derived from a Cree word for fat. Lean meat was sliced thin and dried, generally in warm sun and wind but, if necessary, inside the teepee where it might incidentally become smoked, or in dry, frosty winter air, or, if speed were essential, over a slow fire. The dried meat was pounded into shreds. It was then mixed with melted suet, so that every shred was filmed with fat, and stored in rawhide bags, usually made of the hide of the animal which furnished the meat, chiefly buffalo and caribou. The mouth of the bag was sewn up and every seam sealed with tallow. The bags, for convenience in packing, were supposed to weigh about ninety pounds apiece. If properly made, it lasted indefinitely. Pemmican made in the autumn could not be as carefully dried as summer pemmican, nor did it need to be if intended for consumption in the ensuing winter. Pemmican could spoil if, made in this way, it was kept until the next summer. There is abundant testimony that summer pemmican, properly dried, could be kept for as long as twenty years.

It goes without saying that a food requiring so much labour to prepare was eaten only when supplies of fresh meat or fish ran out. We shall see presently with what care Mackenzie conserved his pemmican against emergencies.

The first third of Mackenzie's *Voyages* is devoted to a description of the fur trade. Only against this background do the great journeys and the explorer's motives and tactics make any sense. 'I was led', he says, 'at an early period of life, by commercial views, to the country north-west of Lake Superior, in North America, and being endowed by nature with an inquisitive mind and enterprising spirit; possessing also a constitution and frame of body equal to the most arduous undertakings, and being familiar with toilsome exertions in the prosecution of mercantile pursuits, I not only contemplated the practicability of penetrating across the continent of America, but was confident in the qualifications, as I was animated by the desire, to undertake the perilous enterprise. The general utility of such a discovery, has been universally acknowledged; while the wishes of my particular friends and commercial associates, that I should proceed in the pursuit of it, contributed to quicken the execution of this favourite project of my own ambition: and as the completion of it extends the boundaries of geographic science, and adds new countries to the realms of British commerce, the dangers I have encountered, and the toils I have suffered, have found their recompense; nor will the many tedious and weary days, or the gloomy and inclement nights which I have passed, have been passed in vain.'

Underneath this somewhat stilted language (for which Mackenzie himself may not be responsible) there is a close-knit chain of thought. As a man whose vocation was trading, he moved boldly into unknown regions, thereby adding to geographical knowledge and to Britain's realms of influence, which were a means of extending British trade. To the extent therefore that we enquire into the fur trade, we are enquiring into Mackenzie's mind and motives.

The fur traders of New France, before the colony was ceded to Britain in 1763, had penetrated to the prairie region beyond the Great Lakes and were trading in the valley of the

Saskatchewan River about as far as the present western boundary of Manitoba. After several years of disruption, following the conquest of New France, its cession to Britain, and the withdrawal to France of too many of its leaders—commercial as well as military, civil and religious—the fur trade from Montreal was resumed by British interests. This enterprise, based on the St Lawrence and Great Lakes, was entirely separate from the Hudson's Bay Company and often in conflict with it.

As to the rapid extension of territory from which furs were taken, we have a vivid and revealing comment from the pen of David Thompson, the explorer.

'Formerly the Beavers were very numerous, the many Lakes and Rivers gave them ample space, and the poor Indian had then only a pointed stick shaped and hardened in the fire, a stone Hatchet, Spear and Arrow-heads of the same; thus armed he was weak against the sagacious Beaver who on the banks of a Lake made itself a house of a foot thick or more; composed of earth and small flat stones, crossed and bound together with pieces of wood; upon which no impression could be made but by fire. But when the arrival of the White People had changed all their weapons from stone to iron and steel and added the fatal Gun, every animal fell before the Indian. The Beaver became a desirable animal for food and clothing, and the fur a valuable article of trade; and as the Beaver is a stationary animal, it could be attacked at any convenient time in all seasons, and thus their numbers soon became reduced.

'For the furrs which the Natives traded, they procured from the French, Axes, Chissels, Knives, Spears and other articles of iron, with which they made good hunts of fur-bearing animals and procured woollen clothing. Thus armed the houses of the Beavers were pierced through, the Dams

27

cut through, and the water of the Ponds lowered, or wholly run off, and the houses of the Beaver and their Burrows laid dry, by which means they became an easy prey to the Hunter.'

In return for his furs, the Indian needed arms, ammunition, cloth and cooking utensils; he also wanted such things as vermilion, tobacco, beads and liquor. Traders' lists include Witney blankets, 'Strouds' (which were large coarsely woven blankets made for the North American trade), 'Coatings, Moltons, serges and Flannel, common Blue and Scarlet cloths'. These woollens came from Yorkshire; Manchester supplied cottons. We find listed, 'Striped Cottons, Dimities, Janes, Fustians, Printed British Cottons, Shawls and Handkerchiefs, Gartering and Ferretting'. We find Irish linens, Scotch sheetings, nets, twine, thread, worsted yarn; 'cutlery and ironmongery', 'kettles of brass and copper and sheetiron'; 'twist and carrot tobacco'; and always, of necessity, 'Pistols, Powder, Ball, Shot and Flints' and Birmingham 'hardware'. Food and liquor came chiefly from the settled parts of Canada, and some Indian corn from the United States. There was no need for these to cross the Atlantic.

As the fur trade was reorganized in the 1760's, following the fall of New France, we find some French traders being guaranteed by British capital, and increasing numbers of Scots moving into the west as partners or employees of new firms. A vivid description survives, of actual operations at this time.

'The adventurer in the Indian Trade must have his Goods ready at Montreal in the *Month of April* consequently they must be arrived from England at Quebec in or before the Month of Novem the preceding year, from there during the winter they must be transported to Montreal where they are prepared for the Indian Voyage by being put up in Packages, not exceeding One hundred pounds weight each, and every package is, or should be, an assortment of different species of Merchandize. These Packages are then conveyed in carts to a place call^d La Chine three leagues further up the River than Montreal, to avoid the Falls of St Lewis situated between these two places; there the Birch canoes with their complement of 6 men each, being ready, the Goods are put on board and so they proceed (the first week in May) on the voyage by the River Ottawaes to the Post of Michilimakinac about 300 Leagues west of Montreal.

'As they must unload and Land their Canoes every night and during the course of the Voyage carry them on their backs in 35 different places some of which are a league long it is generally from 35 to 40 days after their departure from La Chine before they arrive at Michilimakinac.

'This Indian Post has long been famous for its convenient situation between the Great Lakes and therefore the constant rendezvous of the Canadian Traders in particular. Here they unload their large Canoes and put the Goods into lesser ones which are despatched to different places on and about the Lakes Huron, Superior and Michigan.

'It is generally the middle of June before the Earliest Canoes arrives, the remainder of this Month, July, August, and September, is all the time the traders have to dispose of their Goods and to carry their furs to Montreal, if in this time they cannot finish their Business, and are obliged to stay all winter, they are sure to make a loseing voyage.'[1]

In the account of Mackenzie's voyages which follows, I have tried to preserve the flavour and texture of things by keeping fairly close to his own style. This, however, involves

---

[1] This account is taken from a contemporary document, now in the Canadian Archives, and is quoted in H. A. Innis's *The Fur Trade in Canada*.

some verbal tactics which should be explained to the reader in advance. The volume through which the world came to know Mackenzie was published in London in 1801 and entitled *Voyages from Montreal through the Continent of North America to the Frozen and Pacific Oceans in 1789 and 1793*. It opens with a lengthy account of the fur trade, written by Roderick Mackenzie, Alexander's cousin. The story of the actual journeys, although this is nowhere indicated, comes from the pen of William Combe. He was a reputable writer, the author of the immensely popular stories of 'Dr Syntax', and he had already written up for publication the *Voyages* of John Meares, published in 1790. As we have Mackenzie's own journal (recopied, but probably quite faithfully) for the journey to the Arctic, it is possible to see to what extent Combe distorted the narrative. In fact, he did very well by it, for the most part contenting himself with imparting a fashionable elegance to Mackenzie's direct phrases. 'Mr Leroux got his men and Indians to salute us with several Vollies to which we returned a few Shot' is Mackenzie's phrasing and differentiates rather urgently the party close to base, able to fire 'vollies', from the party in the canoes, already intent on the journey and unwilling to waste powder on more than a few token discharges. Combe's version loses this realism: 'We were saluted on our departure with some vollies of small arms, which we returned.' A few pages farther on, Mackenzie remarks, 'The Indians complain much of our hard Marching, that they are not accustomed to such hard fatigue.' Combe has it that 'the Indians complained of the perseverance with which we pushed forward, and that they were not accustomed to such severe fatigue as it occasioned'. Frequently we find a bit of phrasing that looks like Combe but is actually in the original. Combe writes, 'We made them smoke, though it was evident they did not know the use of tobacco; we likewise supplied them with grog; but I am disposed to think that they accepted our civilities rather from fear than inclination.' This is hardly altered from Mackenzie's record, 'we made them smoak, tho' it was evident they did not know the use of Tobacco, we likewise gave them some Grog to drink, but I believe they accepted of those Civilities more through Fear than Inclination'. As Mackenzie, moreover, put his own name on the title-page of Combe's rendition, we may on all counts assume that it was fairly close to what he himself would have produced as a final version if he could have spared the time and effort for the task.

The reader should keep in mind, then, that during the journey north to the Arctic we are closely following Mackenzie's journal and at intervals quoting from it, while during the journey west to the Pacific, for which Mackenzie's journal does not seem to have survived, we are similarly following and quoting from Combe. For reasons just suggested, the reader will not find it difficult to move from one to the other. Brief quotations, which shift, naturally, into the first person, are introduced where it seems they will bring with them the feeling of Mackenzie's actual voice and presence.

In considering what to do with the eighteenth-century prose of Mackenzie and Combe, the present writer has been surprised to find that, to use a current phrase, 'the medium is the message'. To translate Mackenzie's sentences into twentieth-century wording is to falsify them. On the northern journey, he tried to climb one of a range of mountains which look much closer to the river than they in fact are. With one of his Indians he started off and after three hours of walking through bush and up the lower slopes they seemed as far away as ever from their goal. Mackenzie's journal entry concludes: 'My Companion wanted absolutely to return, his Shoes and leggins were all torn to Pieces, besides he said that we wou'd not be able to return thro' such bad Road in the Night, however I persisted in proceeding & that we wou'd pass the Night in the Mountains & return in the Morning, as we approach'd them the grd became quite Marshy & we waded in Water & Grass up to the Middle till we came within a Mile of the Foot of the Mountains, where I fell in up to the Arm Pits & with some difficulty extricated myself, I found it impossible to proceed in a Str. Line & the Marsh extended as far as I could see, so that I did not attempt to make the Circuit, so therefore thought it most prudent to make the best of my Way back to my Canoe (tho it was Night when I arriv'd after 12 oClk very much fatigued.' The immediacy of this record is lost in any précis or paraphrase, together with the balance between Mackenzie's rational, concrete grasp of things and his inexorable drive toward achievement.

The problem presented by Mackenzie's style is present also in his arrangement of the events in the course of his journeys. We are tempted to look for turning points and climaxes, for significant crises toward which the story builds and from which it descends. These can be found, if we look for them; it is clear, however, that Mackenzie thinks only in terms of progress toward his goal. A smashed canoe and lost ammunition are viewed simply as hindrances to his journey. Each day is significant, not for the events it brings but for the distance covered toward the far-off objective. Once we identify ourselves with this man and feel as he feels, the narrative shapes itself. We add day to day, like beads on a string, till the whole is clasped by the quietly triumphant return to point of departure. There are no gaps or lapses, few delays, only one brief bit of back tracking, not even decisive pauses between outward and return journey. The energy of onward movement is sustained; progress may be slowed but is never halted; the organized effort of will prevails.

I

Lake Athabasca and Peter Pond

ALEXANDER MACKENZIE's first voyage took him down the whole length of the river named after him, to where its waters reached the Arctic Ocean. The second also brought him to salt water, this time to the far west, on the shores of a deep inlet from the Pacific. His starting point for both expeditions was Lake Athabasca, a sheet of cold water of more than 3,000 square miles just south of the 60th parallel of latitude. On a modern map it is seen to lie across the boundary between Alberta and Saskatchewan. It is still, to this day, a long way from anywhere.

Into the south-west corner of Lake Athabasca flows the Athabasca River. In a small log-built trading post on its bank two men spent a great part of the winter of 1787–8, discussing plans to increase the fur trade in this wild and remote region. Both were members of the North West Company, an active rival to the old Hudson's Bay Company. Alexander Mackenzie, the young Scotsman of twenty-four, had come north to replace Peter Pond, who at forty-eight was getting old for a fur trader and would soon retire to his native United States. We can be reasonably certain what the two of them talked about during the long snowbound months before a wood fire that never went out.

Mackenzie appears to have been of medium height, wiry and resilient, with a fresh complexion and a resolute expression. Lawrence's portrait (see frontispiece) is undoubtedly idealized but it answers so well to what we know of Mackenzie and is, in its traits, so faithful to the Highland type of the Mackenzie clan that we can accept it confidently as a good likeness. It suggests neither arrogance nor rashness but the perfection of self-reliance.

How many men were under Pond's direction, from this central trading post of the region, it is impossible to know. Exclusive of Indians loosely associated with the operation, they may have numbered four or five score. They do not seem to have entered into the counsels of the two leaders.

Peter Pond, who was born in 1740, in Connecticut, which still owed allegiance to the Crown, was a self-educated and, in all respects, self-made man. That we know nothing of his external appearance seems of little account, so powerfully does his personality project itself in action. He was a man of extraordinary energy—proud, ambitious and enterprising. We hear a good deal about him from men who were his rivals and enemies. But his achievements speak for themselves. He was the first white man known to have reached the Athabasca country and he organized lines of transport that brought the whole of this new and rich area to the fur trading system. As an explorer he was limited by his duties and by his lack of navigation instruments. What he will always be remembered for are his pioneer maps of the north-west. These were strange examples of cartography. They relied heavily upon stories told by Indians who were often merely repeating what they had heard. Pond was a past master at picking up this kind of information but, naturally, much of it was vague and unreliable. Yet, if his maps were generally inaccurate, they were brilliant feats of the imagination. They amalgamated established facts, such as the location of Lake Superior or Hudson's Bay, with Pond's own knowledge of Lake Athabasca and Great Slave Lake, and with Indian reports of waterways leading northward into the tundra and reaching tidal water. Lake Athabasca he calls Lake of the Hills and marks it as 'discover'd by P. Pond 1776'. The eastern end of Great Slave Lake bears the legend 'much ice July 1787'. At 100° N. latitude he sketches a vague coastline and notes, 'Here the water ebbs and flows according to the account of the Natives and they know of no land further to the Northward.' He evidently thought this northern cold sea to be a possible way out to the Pacific.

It was in his attempts to fill in from Lake Athabasca to the west that Pond's maps were principally misleading. He seems to have been uncertain whether the river draining Great Slave Lake flowed westward toward the Pacific or northward into the Arctic. The map he prepared in July, 1787, for presentation to the Empress of Russia shows Great Slave Lake drained by a great river flowing due west, toward the inlet of the Pacific discovered and explored by Captain Cook. That Pond believed the former to flow into the latter is apparent from the following notation printed in the blank between them: 'Capt. Cook found the water on this Coast to be much fresher than Salt or Sea water: also a quantity of drift wood no doubt carried thither by the Rivers Araubaska, Peace and Mountain as they commonly overflow their banks in the months of May and August, the former owing to the breaking up of Ice and the latter to the great quantity of Snow upon the Mountains melting about that time and at each of these periods there arrives down a vast quantity of large wood such as is not to be met with to the Northward of the above mention'd Rivers.'

In addition to the map prepared for the Empress Catherine, Pond in 1785 produced two others, one for the American Congress and the other for Lord Hamilton, who sent it to England. One cannot avoid the impression, in looking at these maps, that Pond was presenting his case to three possible patrons in three different forms, each nicely calculated to rouse the interest of the recipient. The map intended for consumption in London shows a great network of lakes and rivers extending from Hudson's Bay and Lake Superior, on the east, to Athabasca Lake in the far north-west, and beyond right up to the 'Ice Sea' or Arctic. The west coast is shown as only some four hundred miles from Lake Athabasca and it looks as though it could be reached without much difficulty.

The map made up for Russian consumption places what is now Alaska in the middle, between the Russian territories of Siberia and 'Kampschatka', on one side, and the network of waterways already referred to, on the other. The whole north-west of America appears to lie open to Russian penetration.

The third map, designed for consumption in Washington, is not concerned with anything on the Pacific side of the mountains, but focuses attention on the ease with which— either from Hudson's Bay or from the Great Lakes or from the headwaters of the Mississippi—it is possible for Americans to move right up to the Arctic, here labelled 'Mer du Nord West'.

If these maps merely demonstrated Peter Pond's skill as a salesman, they would be nothing more than amusing curiosities. But, in fact, they reveal with startling clarity three possible destinies for what is now western Canada—to fall under Russian domination, to become part of the United States of America, or to be held within the sphere of British control and associated with 'Canada' as it then was, lying east of the Great Lakes.

The maps themselves provoked no immediate response. On 1 March, 1785, his earliest known map was presented to

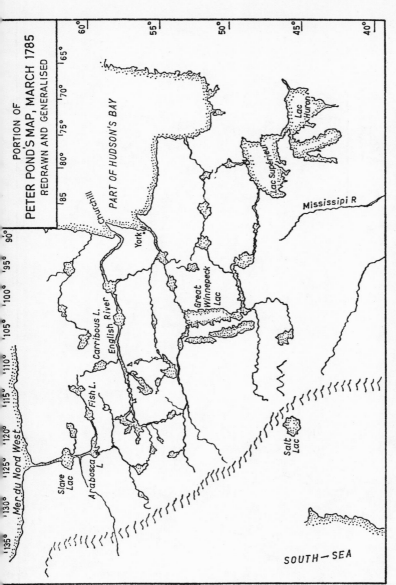

PORTION OF
PETER POND'S MAP, MARCH 1785
REDRAWN AND GENERALISED

60°
55°
50°
45°
40°

65°
70°
75°
80°
85°
90°
95°
100°
105°
110°
115°
120°
125°
130°
135°

PART OF HUDSON'S BAY

Churchill

York

Lac Huron

Lac Supérieur

Mississipi R

Great Winnepeck Lac

Carribous L.

English River

Fish L.

Slave Lac

Arabosca L.

Mer du Nord West

Salt Lac

SOUTH—SEA

Based on map presented to the American Congress by Peter Pond, March, 1785

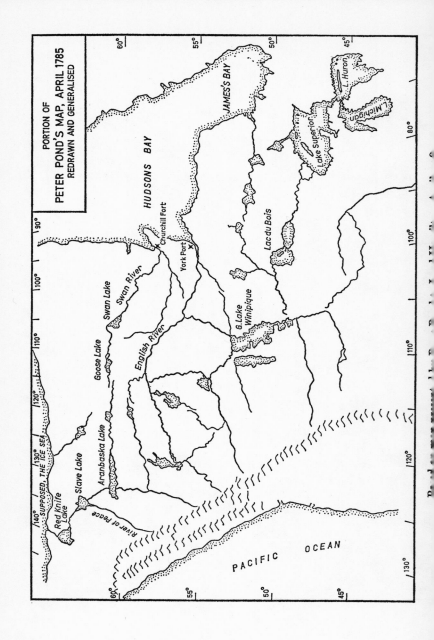

PORTION OF
PETER POND'S MAP, APRIL 1785
REDRAWN AND GENERALISED

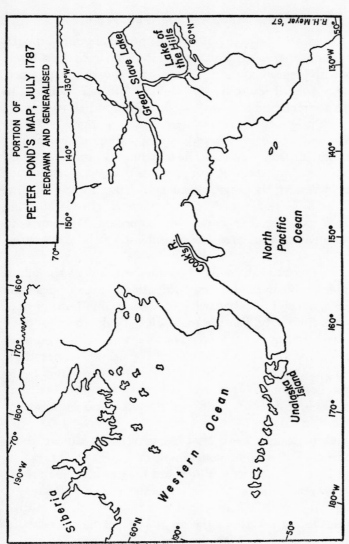

PORTION OF
PETER POND'S MAP, JULY 1787
REDRAWN AND GENERALISED

Great Slave Lake

Lake of
the Hills

60°N

130°W

140°

150°

70°

160°

170°

180°

190°W

70°

60°N

90°

50°

Siberia

Western Ocean

Unalaska Island

North
Pacific
Ocean

Cook's R.

R.H.Meyer '67

130°W

140°

150°

160°

170°

180°W

50°N

Based on map prepared by Peter Pond for presentation to the Empress of Russia, July, 1787 the American Congress but without producing any support. Very soon afterwards Pond appears to have had an interview with Henry Hamilton, Lieutenant-Governor of Quebec, who on 9 April wrote to the Colonial Office in London, in warm appreciation of Pond's work, and promised to forward the map prepared for them together with a digest of Pond's views about the west. There is no indication of any favourable response from London. The map made in 1787, to be laid before the Empress of Russia, reveals that Pond had somewhat increased his geographical knowledge in the interval but there is no record of its having reached Catherine II. It is possible that Pond, who expected Mackenzie to traverse Russia and so reach England, intended the map to go by his hand.

These maps or others like them must have been spread on the plank table in the trading post with an outlook across the frozen surface of Athabasca River. Living conditions were of rigorous simplicity, fish the main diet, a cake made of flour a luxury, brandy or tobacco or powder and ball for hunting all measured out with care. Wood for firing was plentiful; fish or game when frozen kept indefinitely; there could be no shortage of water. There were not many Indians about but relations were friendly, skins were traded and Pond's men were not inactive.

Mackenzie must have heard a good deal, during these months of close contact, concerning Peter Pond's earlier life, about his adroitness as a trader and his never to be fulfilled desire to reach the northern and western oceans. Pond was so important to Mackenzie and the groundwork he laid so essential to the success of the great voyages that we should listen to his story, as Mackenzie would have heard it and as the elder man was later to write it down.

He had been born in Connecticut, in 1740, the son of a

shoemaker, and did not spend much time in school. At sixteen he wanted to join the army but his parents forbade him;
there was a large young family to look after. He enlisted,
nevertheless, and by the time he was twenty had fought in
two campaigns against the French and earned his commission. We may imagine Mackenzie hearing with interest the
stories of battles fought before he was born, in much the same
phrasing as Pond afterwards set down in his memoirs.

In 1758, in the old pre-revolutionary days, Pond found
himself as a loyal colonial under the command of General
James Abercromby, whose mixed force of British and
American troops launched an attack on Ticonderoga. This
fort had been strategically sited by the French on a pro-
montory at the south end of Lake Champlain and Pond
recalled an armada of over a thousand boats, together with
a floating battery and gunboats proceeding up the lakes. It
was all in vain. The French were commanded by Montcalm
—who was later to face Wolfe at Quebec—and the attack,
made for some reason without the support of the artillery,
failed disastrously. Pond summed it up as the 'Most Ridicklas
Campane Eaver Hard of'. But the next year saw the historic
battle of the plains of Abraham, the fall of Quebec and the
isolation of Montreal. Pond, who now held a commission, was
again on active service, with Amherst's army that reached
Montreal and received its surrender.

When the war that gave Britain possession of New France
was over, Peter Pond turned to civilian pursuits. His father,
who died in 1764, had been for some time engaged in fur
trading and the son perhaps followed in his footsteps. He
made two lengthy expeditions into the upper valley of the
Mississippi and showed himself adept at dealing with the
Indians, even those who had never traded with a white man,
and with tribes on the brink of war, to whom he went as a

peacemaker. He learned to cope with boatmen, honest and dishonest, to exist in harsh climates and dangerous situations and to make friends even of rivals trading in the same territory. In the summer of 1775 he decided to try the route that led through Lake Superior to Grand Portage and the northwest.

His reasons were those of a thoroughly practical man. Although New York was a greater centre of business and shipping, he found it easier to get certain goods in Montreal. This was not surprising; the Montreal fur trade, now being expanded by British interests, had developed a detailed knowledge of what the Indians wanted. More important, the finest furs came from further north than the Mississippi valley, because the climate was more rigorous. Competition, moreover, was less strenuous in the north, even allowing for the presence of the Hudson's Bay Company. And, finally, it is probable that Pond sensed the oncoming war between Britain and the thirteen colonies. The Boston Tea Party had taken place some eighteen months before and, as Pond, on his new expedition, took his canoes through Grand Portage and on to Lake Winnipeg in June of 1775, the phrasing of the Declaration of Independence, which would appear a year later, must already have been shaping itself in the mind of Thomas Jefferson. Whatever happened, there would be no fighting or disruption of trade in the enormous, largely unexplored north-west into which Pond was now hopefully moving.

He built a post on the Saskatchewan River and seems to have maintained a trade even against the Hudson's Bay Company, which proceeded to build still farther upstream. But it was clear that a magnificent untouched territory lay still farther to the north-west and for the exploitation of this virgin field Pond was peculiarly well equipped. His long experience had made him mobile and resourceful; his knowledge of men had been gained in a school of hard experience; his command of the techniques of transportation by canoe must have been nearly flawless. One of these techniques was the provision of food for large crews of hard-paddling and portaging voyageurs. They could carry only a limited supply with them and they moved so fast there was little time for hunting and fishing. When we come to follow Mackenzie's own day-by-day experience on his great expeditions, we shall find how constantly he had to think of food.

A trader named Thomas Frobisher had shown in 1776 that it was possible to spend the winter as far up as Isle à la Crosse Lake and find there a good supply of fish. He had hoped to get even farther, to Lake Athabasca, but he had not managed it. There was every reason for a trader adept at canoe travel to try again, for in these upper regions, where no large rivers, like the Saskatchewan, flowed toward Hudson's Bay, the old Company was at a disadvantage as it tended to rely on boats and established routes.

Accordingly, Pond determined to strike out for the Athabasca region and, typically, he found fellow traders who showed confidence in him. All this he told to the young Mackenzie, as the interminable winter drifted about the wooden walls of their hut. We have the story from Mackenzie himself or, to be quite accurate, from the pen of his cousin Roderick who wrote 'A general history of the fur trade', published as an introduction to the *Voyages*. It is a brief account in which each sentence fills in some important detail. It opens with a reference to Thomas Frobisher.

'The success of this gentleman induced others to follow his example and in the spring of the year 1778 some of the traders on the Saskatchiwine river finding they had a quantity of goods to spare agreed to put them into a joint

43

stock, and gave the charge and management of them to Peter Pond, who, in four canoes, was directed to enter the English River, so called by Mr. Frobisher, to follow his track, and proceed still further; if possible to Athabaska, a country hitherto unknown but from an Indian report. . . . Here he passed the winter of 1778–9; saw a vast concourse of the Knisteneaux and Chepewyan tribes, who used to carry their furs annually to Churchill the latter by the barren grounds, where they suffered innumerable hardships and were sometimes even starved to death. The former followed the course of the lakes and rivers, through a country that abounded in animals, and where there was plenty of fish; but though they did not suffer from want of food, the intolerable fatigue of such a journey could not be easily repaid to an Indian, they were therefore highly gratified by seeing people come to their country to relieve them from such long toilsome and dangerous journies; and were immediately reconciled to give an advanced price for the article necessary to their comfort and convenience. Mr. Pond's reception and success was accordingly beyond his expectation, and he procured twice as many furs as his canoes would carry. They also supplied him with as much provision as he required during his residence among them and sufficient for his homeward voyage. Such of the furs as he could not embark, he secured in one of his winter huts and they were found the following season, in the same state in which he left them.'

It seems certain that Mackenzie and Pond, after a winter together, were on amicable terms, though they had not become close friends. Pond was not all sweetness and light. In the spring of 1782, after he had passed the winter with a trader named Waden, the two had had a quarrel and Waden, receiving a bullet in his leg, died from loss of blood. Pond and a clerk were tried for murder in Montreal and were acquitted. During the winter of 1786–7, a rival trader named John Ross was killed and the news spread that he 'had been shot in a scuffle with Mr Pond's men'. It was actually this event which brought Pond and Mackenzie together. It was so startlingly clear that a fratricidal strife among traders would ruin them all that, very hastily, the North West Company, which Pond had joined a couple of years earlier, took in a number of smaller enterprises and thus acquired the services of Mackenzie, who received one share in the Company and was sent up to Athabasca to replace the fractious Pond.

In the spring of 1788 Pond came down to Montreal and in 1790 returned to Milford, Connecticut. He died in 1807. As historians sift the record, they find the evidence against him rather uncertain, in connection with the deaths of Waden and Ross; as the facts of his achievement are established, his role in the operations leading to Mackenzie's ultimate triumph appears ever larger and more significant.

The young Mackenzie's personal relations with Pond at this time seem to have been cordial enough, which is a tribute to both of them. It cannot have been pleasant for a veteran trader to be replaced by someone half his age, especially when his own future was uncertain. On the other side, it must have been difficult for Mackenzie to conceal his dislike of Pond's carelessness—he was repeatedly associated with violent acts of a kind which Mackenzie strove by every possible means to avoid; he was vague in his handling of geographic knowledge, whereas Mackenzie tried hard for precision; he was not a reliable reporter of facts. When he reached Quebec he had some long conversations with a clerk of the Crown named Isaac Ogden, who wrote an account of them to his father in London. This is full of misinformation: the longitude of the western end of Great Slave

Lake is given as 134° west and the mouth of 'Cook's River' on the Pacific as 154°. This makes the distance as the crow flies to be about 650 miles, whereas it is in fact about 1,100 miles. Nor was Pond very accurate about Mackenzie. Ogden's letter to his father in London continues, 'Another man by the name of McKenzie was left by Pond at Slave Lake with orders to go down the River, and from thence to Unalaska, and so to Kamskatsha, and thence to England through Russia, &c. If he meets with no accident, you may have him with you next year.' This bristles with inaccuracies, most of which must have been Pond's. Far from being under orders, Mackenzie was acting largely on his own initiative. Far from having an assured course to the Pacific he was separated from it by a mass of mountains which embodied a continental divide. As for reaching England via Russia, the vision of Mackenzie's voyageurs paddling merrily down the Lena River and, after many portages, up the Volga, has its own charm; or perhaps he was to go on alone, like Defoe's Crusoe crossing Russia, and leave his men to find their own way home.

At any rate, we are able to judge of the difference in character and temperament between the two men, to admire Pond's enterprise and wide-ranging imagination, to be glad that Mackenzie took over at this critical juncture, and to see why the two had much to talk about as the long cold days and sub-arctic nights went by. One bids farewell to Peter Pond with reluctance. All accounts agree that he died in poverty and without recognition. He deserved better.

During that winter, Mackenzie probably had far less to say than Pond but he must have conveyed, bit by bit, his own straightforward career up to that point. He had been born in Stornoway in 1764. His clan took its origin in Kintail and its name from a thirteenth-century chief named Kenneth. It became wealthy and powerful in the fifteenth century and probably rose to the height of its influence during the reign of James VI. After that, the Civil War, which prolonged itself into the Jacobite risings, was the cause of many losses. Some families in the Mackenzie connection have possessed wide political powers. Both Kintail and Cromartie houses were able to raise their own regiments.

Expansion brought the clan to the west coast, first under the protection of the Earls of Ross, with whom they had a blood tie, and later, after the Ross estates were forfeited to the Crown in 1476, in their own right. The chiefs early owned land in the Long Island, the northernmost of the Outer Hebrides, now known as Lewis. When, in 1623, the head of the clan was created Earl of Seaforth, he took this title from a sea loch in the island. It is a reflection on the times that Mackenzie of Kintail, as he was called from the original home of the clan, should acquire his new earldom on the strength of lands bought up from a group of Lowlanders whom James VI had encouraged to settle on Lewis, to develop its economy and make use of the harbour of Stornoway. The Fife Adventurers, as they were called, made no headway against the lairds and the local clansmen. Lewis retained its ancient order and Mackenzie succeeded in getting a royal charter for the whole island. The clan held lands from one side of Scotland to the other, from Moray Firth on the east to Lewis, in the cold waters of the North Atlantic.

Alexander's father, Kenneth Mackenzie, was an ensign in the Stornoway Company which opposed the Jacobites in 1745. He was of honourable ancestry and married into one of Stornoway's leading families, named Maciver. There were four children—Murdoch, Alexander, Sybilla and Margaret. Alexander was born in a substantial stone house in Stornoway, of which there exists a sketch, but during at least part of his childhood the family lived at Melbost farmhouse, two miles out of the town. We know little of their circumstances. It is probable that they were poor but not impoverished; Murdoch studied medicine and became a ship's surgeon.

In Mackenzie's day, the town of Stornoway was little more than a village, but was even then the centre of the north-western fishing industry and a kind of 'tradesman's entrance' to the Hebrides, through which passed those economic necessities the islemen could not produce for themselves. An atmosphere of commercial exchange must have surrounded the boy from his earliest years.

Many changes have come over Stornoway and its hinter-land since those days. The streets are no longer compounded of clay and rock, or filled with cumbersome carts; the old Town Hall Mackenzie knew has been destroyed by fire; Martin's Memorial Church stands on the corner of Francis and Kenneth Streets where Mackenzie's birthplace stood.

The countryside has also changed. The shielings, which used to provide the crofters with a summer dwelling while the cattle were out on the hill pastures, are now in ruins, mere piles of rough-hewn stones. The crofts, too, have altered. When crofters were all fishermen, the croft house was near the sea. As better farming methods came in, the crofter be-came less dependent on fishing and found it pleasanter to live out of the reach of sea spray, on the landward side of his cultivation. Houses themselves have changed: the 'black house', with its thatch, its built-in byre and henhouse, is gone. The very moor has lost something of its immemorial look: many acres have been reclaimed and reseeded and in places the peat cutters have stripped the surface to bare rock or clay.

Yet much remains the same as in old times, or scarcely altered. The sea never changes. The climate continues to exact an active, hardy, provident way of life. The moor, the deeply indented coast, the rocky hills: these still encourage physical activity and there are old men who remember how, when young, they thought little of setting out from the west side of the island and crossing Barvas moor on foot, to reach a dance on the east side.

The young Alexander's education remains something of a mystery. He shows no signs, in his writing, of having studied the customary Latin classics or of the type of doctrinal instruction we associate with Calvinism. It is even possible that a good many hours of his boyhood were spent in fishing or farm work, to the neglect of formal schooling. In any case, he left Scotland when he was about ten years of age. His family were in no sense peasants and we should remember that his father was an army officer and his brother a qualified surgeon. We must see him coming from the matrix of Scottish society where a sentiment of intense self-reliance, pride and independence subsumes social differences which elsewhere produce class distinctions. Mackenzie may not have been impeccably literate but it is clear that in Quebec and later in England he could meet the Duke of York on terms of comradeship.

At an early age he must have joined in the outdoor activity which has always attracted the boys of Lewis—swimming and diving, ball games and pitch-and-toss, fishing in salmon lochs and trout streams for sport. The market, held in the old days on Markethill near the site of the present War Memorial, combined the functions of a cattle-mart, a fun-fair, a marriage pool and an arena where those with chips on their shoulders could, in the approved manner, settle their differences.

Semi-organized entertainment could be found at the 'ceilidh', a sort of folk-concert, generally held in a private house, where violins and bagpipes were played, songs sung, and stories told. The stories were famous; most of the raconteurs were old sailors who had seen, so they said, all manner of wonders in foreign lands. Here and elsewhere, the young Mackenzie would also imbibe the barbarous, romantic history of the island, where the legendary mystic of the Hebrides, Coinneach Odhar, had been burned alive and where Bonnie Prince Charlie had taken refuge after the disasters of the Forty-five. It is probable that the boy played in the ruins of the earliest Seaforth Castle, situated on the rocks which now support King Edward's wharf. Long afterwards, he was to record, as he began his descent of the Fraser River, that the cliffs of blue and yellow clay reminded him of the ruined walls of old castles, and such references are very rare in his writings.

Stornoway and its people have for centuries exhibited a mingling of Scottish and English traditions and attitudes. Mackenzie's mixed inheritance does not fail to embrace Celtic pride, a Highlander's loyalties, the self-reliance of the Lewismen. Nor is this found incompatible with an equally traditional Scottish caution and foresight. It was Mackenzie's good luck that these capacities, combined with the Stornowegian instinct for trade, should find a wide scope for action in the context of English overseas enterprise, which Scots, after the Act of Union, entered into with such vigour.

An odd, symbolic fact should be noted: the latitude of Mackenzie's fort on Lake Athabasca is precisely that of Stornoway.

Alexander's mother died when he was about ten years old and his father made up his mind to leave Stornoway for New York where the boy had an uncle. A few months after they arrived, the war of American Independence broke out and his father and uncle joined the Loyalists as lieutenants in the

King's Royal Regiment of New York. His father died, perhaps as a prisoner of war, at Carleton Island in Lake
Ontario, in 1780. The boy by this time had, for safety's sake,
been sent to Canada and, after being briefly at school in
Montreal, had begun work, at the age of fifteen, with
Gregory, McLeod and Co. of Montreal, fur traders. The
next five years were passed in their service and by the time
he was twenty he had learned a great deal about the trade
and impressed his employers with his energy and adroitness.
They sent him on a trading mission to Detroit where he
rapidly made contact with Indians in the back country and
avoided conflict with traders already established. He was
immediately offered a partnership in the company on condition that he go out to the north-west next spring, 1785.

Headquarters for the west was at Grand Portage and here
it was decided that, of the partners present, John Ross should
go up to Athabasca, Mackenzie to English River (now known
as Churchill River) and others to other points. Next summer,
Alexander was joined by his cousin Roderick, who had
recently come out from Scotland and joined the company as
a clerk. They were to remain, with one brief interlude, very
warm and loyal friends for the rest of their lives. It was
Roderick who, when he heard that John Ross had been shot
and killed, dashed down to Grand Portage carrying the
news. With five voyageurs, travelling at top speed through
a maze of lakes, rivers and portages, he made the journey of
roughly twelve hundred miles in a month. As we have seen,
the news was so alarming in its threat of mutual destruction
that all concerned suddenly came to their senses and in July of
that year, 1787, the union was effected which brought Mackenzie and his friends into the North West Company. The
one share he received was, from any point of view, a highly
desirable acquisition. He had thoroughly learned the routines

51

of the trade in Montreal; at Detroit he had shown energy, daring and resourcefulness; in his post on the Churchill he had maintained good relations with the North West Company's man, William McGillivray, even though they were in keen competition. He was twenty-four years of age. It is a marvellous tribute to his abilities that he was now chosen to replace Peter Pond in this remote and troubled territory. After a journey which took him up the Churchill, through a long string of lakes, then down the Clearwater, a tributary of the Athabasca, he came to Fort Athabasca on 21 October, 1787. There, as we have seen, he and Peter Pond spent the winter months together.

Pond having returned to Montreal in the spring of 1788, in July Mackenzie went down to Rainy Lake and managed to have his cousin Roderick transferred from English River to his own bailiwick at Athabasca. He needed someone to assist him in a complete reorganization of his district, someone he could trust to hold the fort while he went off on an expedition into the unknown.

Fort Athabasca, where Mackenzie had spent the winter with Pond, was situated on the Athabasca River, about forty miles above Athabasca Lake. In 1785 Pond had established subsidiary posts on Great Slave Lake. Mackenzie was now determined to centralize his operation in a new fort and to abandon Fort Athabasca. He sent Roderick down to the lake, to establish the new post. The site selected was on the south shore, 'about eight miles from the discharge of the river'. It was named Fort Chipewyan (variously spelled) after the Chipewyan Indians whose bands were scattered from Great Slave and Athabasca Lakes to Hudson Bay and from what is now northern Manitoba and northern Saskatchewan as far northward as Eskimo territory.

The new fort commanded a lake filled with fish, a vital

matter in view of the uncertainty of supplies of game and the impossibility of bringing in food sufficient for more than ninety men attached to the post. Here Roderick could control the whole operation, while Alexander went looking for new worlds to conquer.

The strategy and tactics of his assault on the wilderness of the west will become, in the course of our story, reasonably clear. His motivation is less easy to grasp. Even when we reflect on his own character, on the nature of the fur trade in general and on the particular ethos of the North West Company, an element of mystery remains. Yet all three of these are worth a moment's consideration at this point.

His character has two sides, public and personal. He is a national hero of the most simple and undisputed kind. This status is not readily conceded in Canada; all the more remarkable that it should belong to a man who was not born or brought up in the country, who left it as soon as he had made his fortune, who opposed the extension of settlement into the west and who thought of life in the regions with which his fame is now associated as a kind of dreadful exile. The reasons for his fame are nevertheless self-evident. He shares in the immemorial and universal regard accorded to explorers, a class of men whose achievements seem beneficial to mankind, not directly associated with conquest or pillage, and stimulating to the imagination.

To Scottish Canadians he is the type of Scots fortitude and decent success; to all British Canadians he is a symbol of British enterprise; for French-Canadians he is associated with Montreal's great decade, beginning in 1790, when the fur trade brought 'un climat de prospérité'. It is his good fortune to be associated, in the minds of French-Canadians, not with the hard-fistedness of English-speaking fur traders based on Montreal, but rather with such names as Fraser, Vancouver,

Cook, La Vérendrye, Jolliet, Marquette and La Salle, which stir the imagination and quicken the pulse.

His personal temperament seems wholly formed by his tradition, by the ethos of his clan, by the fusion of those elements in Scottish life best calculated to ensure survival under the stress of late eighteenth-century conditions. His relations with other men suggest some Lowland addition of canny moderation and foresight to the traditional Highland virtues. He was self-controlled and farsighted. He was proud, resourceful, determined, alert to opportunity and to danger. He relied instinctively on ties of blood for enduring loyalty.

Mackenzie's thinking has a certain characteristic turn, often repeated, which one learns to identify, after having experienced it in dealing with the Scottish engineers, bank managers and university presidents sown thickly across Canada's terrain. It passes imperceptibly from a preoccupation with the obvious to a projection of boldly imaginative plans. There is no gap or lapse of logic or probability as this transition is made. Rooted in the rigours of the Scottish climate, it appears in characters, of fact and fiction, as far removed as Bruce and Jeannie Deans. Mackenzie's double voyage was an heroically simple thing, without moral ambiguity or political complexity. It was a triumph of individual will in an honourable manner, an engagement in rivalry without hatred. Founded on a desire to extend trade, it rose to a level of heroism not easy to discredit.

Mackenzie was clearly well suited to the fur trade, an operation marked by intense rivalry from its very beginnings. As early as 1613 we find Champlain lamenting the folly of French merchants who set out so early, to forestall their competitors, that they became snared in the ice and who when trading secretly offered the Indians much higher prices than their rivals and so ended by getting the worst of the bargain.

During the first half of the seventeenth century, the Iroquois were engaged in a destructive struggle with more northerly Indians supported by the French, for control of the Ottawa River as a route for furs. The second half of the century saw a prolonged conflict for possession of routes through the Great Lakes and through Hudson's Bay. French expansion into the far west was compressed from two sides, from the north by the Hudson's Bay Company, which was chartered in 1670, and from the south by Iroquois and by Dutch and English traders. In 1683 there is bitter complaint about French *coureurs de bois* who have gone over to the English. At the same time the French traders were competing among themselves and in due course a vicious circle was established, from which there was no escape: military ventures in search of wider areas of trade became even more necessary; poorer furs from some of the areas held, lower prices for furs, and competition from cheaper English goods served to reduce the revenue which supported military operations.

During the War of the Austrian Succession (1740–8), known in American history as King George's War, the French fur traders were almost entirely deprived of goods from France. In 1745, fears were expressed 'that the small quantity of merchandise sent to Niagara as well as to the other posts will discourage the Indians and cause them to go to the English to supply their needs'. There were fears of the trade being 'totally lost next year if our vessel does not arrive in good time'.

The Hudson's Bay Company, though exempt from some troubles which beset trading in the St Lawrence valley, had nevertheless to cope with violent opposition. In 1686, a

French expedition captured three Hudson's Bay forts and they were held until 1693. In 1690, 1694, 1696 and 1714 posts changed hands forcibly, one way or the other. After the capture of Quebec in 1759, the Company was relieved of competition for a moment but in the 1770's a new set of traders from Montreal, financed by new, British capital, began once more to compete with trade based on the Bay. During the American War of Independence, there was naturally a fresh incentive to carry trade into the undisturbed north-west. Peter Pond and Alexander Mackenzie were among those who essayed the new territory.

Seen in relief against this murky background of competition, and of violence, even of outright warfare, Mackenzie's own forms of competitiveness are quite understandable. It is clear that within the accepted canons of his time he treated his rivals, his associates, his paid employees and his Indian helpers with fairness, reasonableness and decency. His relations with Lord Selkirk, which do not belong to the period of his life when he made the great voyages, constitute a lamentable exception.

Mackenzie's personality was also sharpened by the peculiar ethos of the North-Westers. On the unstable foundation of a slaughter of wild animals, they developed an organization remarkable for its *élan*, for the fantastic scope of its activities and for the personal pride of its leaders. It existed for some forty-five years, marked by ceaseless struggle and ending in financial collapse. Yet memorable names and memorable achievements leap to the eye in its record.

One of our best sources of information about the North-Westers is in the pages left by Alexander Ross, a young Scotsman, already mentioned, who came to Canada in 1805, at the age of twenty-two. In 1810 he entered the service of Astor's company and took part in the founding of Fort

Astoria, at the mouth of the Columbia River. When the North-Westers took possession of it in 1813, he joined them as a clerk and, after the merger of 1821, took service with the Hudson's Bay Company. He was able, because of his experience with Astor's Pacific Fur Company, to look at his new masters in 1813 with considerable detachment and penetration. Astor's men had been free and easy in their manners. At meal time they had taken their seats without observing precedence or ceremony, no one caring who sat between him and the head of the table. They all partook of the same food and drink. They left as they had entered, without ceremony. American notions of liberty and equality prevailed.

But now the North-Westers have taken command and the scene changes. Those in charge, the great 'Bourgeois' of the Company, are as careful of rank and place as Chinese Mandarins or Teutonic Knights. From the head of the table, there is a graduation of the Company's servants, down to the casual labour at the foot.

What Ross is recording is more than a matter of table manners. It is a contrast between two different orderings of society. The group of American trappers, who took their pelts wherever they could and sold them wherever they wished, was in sharp contrast to the carefully structured Canadian company. Climate had a good deal to do with the difference: it was harder to come by supplies in Canada and they had to be transported over long distances. The British government had something to do with it: ministers had thought, since the days of the East India Company, in terms of granting monopolies of trade. The protocol of the North-Westers at the height of their success, which they appear to have maintained even on the remote Pacific coast, comes alive in Ross's amusing account.

He remarks that, amid all this ceremony at table, no blessing was ever asked, even on a Sunday, and no blessing fell on the activities of the Company. When tea was poured, there were three pots, in order of the quality of China leaf they contained, and three corresponding qualities of sugar. If wine or spirits appeared after dinner, all those below the head of the table, where the Bourgeois sat, retreated.

Ross was in Upper Canada for a few years, between 1805 and 1810, before he went to the Pacific coast. In Montreal he found the North-Westers predominant. Everywhere they appeared to be held in high regard; the voyageurs had transmitted to French-Canadians in general an enthusiasm for the great Company.

The fur trade itself was based on a cruel and reckless slaughter of wild animals. This becomes very clear when we read between the lines of journals and memoirs left by the traders themselves: 'A good many wolves and foxes were caught by the whites, with hook and line as we catch fish; with this difference, however, that the latter are taken in water, the former on dry land. For this purpose three cod-hooks are generally tied together back to back, baited, and then fixed with a line to the branch of a tree, so that the hooks are suspended in the air at the distance of four or five feet from the ground. To get hold of the bait, the wolf has to leap up, and the moment the hooks catch their hold it finds itself either in a standing or suspended position, which deprives the animal of its strength; neither can it in that posture cut the line; it is generally caught, sometimes dead, sometimes alive.'

Since wolves attacked horses, they were killed as a matter of course and, as wild beasts in general were there simply for the purpose of being shot or trapped, there was no feeling for them if they defended themselves. We read of a wounded bear as a 'vicious animal' filled with 'savage fury'. In the words of the old French song,

> Cet animal est très méchant,
> Quand on l'attaque, il se défend.

David Thompson's account of the destruction of the beaver and his observation that, when the white man 'added the fatal gun, every animal fell before the Indian' has already been mentioned. Another means of hastening the beaver's extermination was the use of steel traps, which according to Thompson began in 1797. Slowly, because they were heavy to carry, their use spread throughout the west.

The driving energy which urged North-Westers across the continent was in large measure a response to the decreasing supply of furs in the old districts, as indiscriminate slaughter thinned out the animal population.

It is Mackenzie's distinction that he turned this single-minded quest for commercial profit into a broader intention having the benefit of his country in view and that his pursuit of his objectives, at every level of activity, was so free of deceit, cruelty and aggression.

His motives for conducting the two voyages seem to have been progressively sharpened by events. The natural desire of a trader to extend the territory of his company's operation was evidently refined, during his winter of conversation over Pond's maps, into a resolve to find a passage to the Pacific and thus complete the circuit of the world back to England. Furs from the north-west would then move either east through Montreal or westward toward China, as costs of transport and availability of markets demanded. Today the huge grain crops of the north-west move in precisely this manner.

Pond was able to point to two rivers (now the Mackenzie

and the Peace), one of which might reach the Pacific at a high latitude, while the other promised a passage through the Rockies. He thus put keys into the younger man's firm hands, to unlock the door to the Orient. He could not be expected to know which one would do the trick.

II

Voyage to the Arctic

MACKENZIE set out from Fort Chipewyan on Lake Athabasca at nine o'clock in the morning of 3 June, 1789. 'The
crew consisted of four Canadians, two of whom were attended
by their wives, and a German; we were accompanied also by
an Indian, who had acquired the title of English Chief, and
his two wives, in a small canoe, with two young Indians; his
followers in another small canoe.'

They were not much hampered by baggage: guns and
ammunition, tents, nets, a small amount of goods, not so
much for trade as 'to ensure us a friendly reception among
the Indians', blankets, some instruments of navigation, a few
bags of pemmican and of corn as emergency rations. It must
be remembered that everything, canoes included, had to be
carried by main force over the rough portages.

The names of the voyageurs were Charles Ducette,
Francois Barrieau, Joseph Landry, Pierre de Lorme and John
Steinbruick. The Indian named English Chief had been
attached to Hearne's expedition to Coppermine River in
1772 and had encouraged the Indians of the Athabaska
region to trade their furs at Fort Churchill.

Accompanying the expedition as far as Great Slave Lake
was a canoe in charge of Le Roux, one of the Company's
clerks. In this first stage of the journey, his canoe carried a
good deal of their goods and supplies.

The canoes moved to the western extremity of Lake

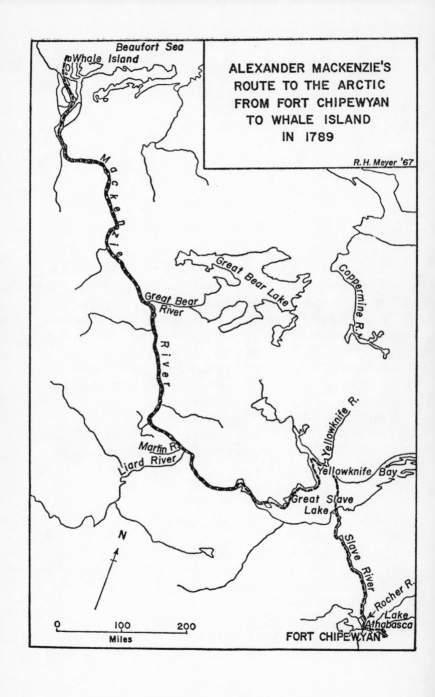

Beaufort Sea
Whale Island

ALEXANDER MACKENZIE'S
ROUTE TO THE ARCTIC
FROM FORT CHIPEWYAN
TO WHALE ISLAND
IN 1789

R. H. Meyer '67

Mackenzie

Great Bear Lake

Coppermine R.

Great Bear River

River

Yellowknife R.

Martin R.

Liard River

Yellowknife Bay

Great Slave Lake

Slave River

N

Rocher R.

Lake Athabasca

0   100   200

Miles

FORT CHIPEWYAN

Athabasca and entered a stream known as Rivière de Quatre Fourches or Rocher River, which joins the lake to the mouth of the Peace River. As Mackenzie observes, it reverses its normal flow when Spring freshets swell the waters of the Peace causing them to flood back into the lake.

It was hard going; the weather was wretched and their progress, in open canoes and totally exposed, was painful.

Sunday, 7 June: 'raining for some time it came on so hard that we were obliged to land and unload to prevent our goods getting wet, in an hours time it cleared up, and we reloaded and got underway, steered N. 10 Miles W. ½ Mile N. 1½ Mile, the rain came on again and obliged us to put in Shore for the Night, about ½ past 3 P.M. we had a strong N.N.E. wind all Day which hindered us much, Mr Leroux's People passed not finding this Place agreeable, the Men and Indians killed 2 Geese and 2 Ducks, rained the rest of the Day.'

Monday, 8 June: 'It blew exceeding hard with rain all last Night and this Day till 2 in the afternoon when the Rain subsided, but the Wind unlimited which prevented our moving this Day.'

At last they reached the point—only some thirty miles in a direct line from Fort Chipewyan—where the Peace River, upwards of a mile broad, pours into (or becomes) the Slave River and turns north. Its current, Mackenzie remarks, is stronger than that of the channel which communicates with the lake.

On Tuesday, 9 June, the expedition arrived at Great Slave Lake, after a good deal of trouble with ice, with driftwood and, above all, with rapids. He had portaged six times and lost a canoe. His grammar is shaken by the event: 'one of the Indian Canoes went down the Fall, but was lucky enough to jump out of her, she was broke to Pieces lost all her Menage.' The weather was also against them.

Great Slave Lake, when they reached it, was covered with ice except along the shore. But the cold at least relieved them of the 'Muskettows and Gnatts' which had been all too thick along the river. With some difficulty, because they were inside a sand bank and in shallow water, they paddled on for five miles and reached 'the houses erected by Messrs Grant and Le Roux in 1786'. Le Roux himself was already there, having gone ahead, two days earlier, making for this spot which was familiar to him.

Here the expedition paused, held up by the ice. It was 29 June before Mackenzie actually got clear of the lake and entered the great stream he had come to explore and which now bears his name. His journal of the intervening days is full of entries recording bad weather, the killing of game and successive attempts to find a passage. His brief notations give us glimpses of the country itself, chilly and inhospitable, the lake still icebound in June; and of the abundance of fish and game which alone made life possible for men.

Tuesday, 9 June: 'upon either side the River the Banks are well covered with all the Kinds of Wood peculiar to this Country, particularly the West side, the land being lower and a richer soil (black Earth) on the East side, the Banks are high, the soil is yellow Clay and Sand, so that the wood is not so big nor so numerous, the Ground is not yet thawed above 18 Inches deep, notwithstanding the Leaf is at its full Growth, tho' there is hardly the appearance of any yet along the Lake—The Indians tell me that at a very little distance on both Sides the River are very extensive Plains, where there are vast Herds of Buffaloes, and that the *Moose* Deer and the largest kind of Rain Deer keep in the Wood close by the River, the Beaver (which are numerous) build their Houses in small Lakes, and Rivers, which they cannot do in the larger River as the Ice carries every thing along with it in the Spring all the Banks of the River are covered with Wild Fowl, We killed 2 Swans 10 Geese 1 Beaver this Morning without losing an hour's time, so that if we were for the purpose of hunting we might soon fill our Canoe.'

Mackenzie's 'reindeer' or 'raindeer' were caribou, which are closely related to reindeer of the Eastern Hemisphere. Woodland and mountain caribou are larger than those of the Arctic tundra and may weigh as much as 700 pounds. Caribou wander widely in search of food and in Mackenzie's day huge herds, numbering more than a thousand, were not uncommon. It was natural for him to use the name he was accustomed to, for animals so similar to the European reindeer. It appears, from his journal entry of 21 June, that he heard his men call them 'carribo'.

Wednesday, 10 June: 'Rained for the greatest part of the last Night and this day till the afternoon, which has weakened the Ice much.'

Thursday, 11 June: 'Strong Westerly Winds fine clear weather, the Women went to gather Berries, of which they brought us many (Say Cramberries) and are very plentiful in this Country—went with one of the Men to a small Island close bye where we picked up some Dozens of Swan, Geese and Duck Eggs, and killed a Brace of Ducks and a Goose . . . The Ice moved a little to the Eastward.'

Friday, 12 June: 'The Weather as Yesterday towards Noon our old Companions (the Muskettoes) visit us in greater Numbers than we would wish as they are very troublesome Guests, the Ice moved again in the same Direction, I ascended a Hill close by, but could not perceive that the Ice had been broke in the Middle of the Lake. Hunters killed a Goose and 3 Ducks.'

Saturday, 13 June: 'Cloudy Weather, the Wind change-able about Sun Set it settled in the N.E. and drove back the

Ice much broken along shore, and covered our Netts. One of the Hunters that had been at the Grand River since last Night came back with 3 Beavers and 14 Geese, he was accompanied by 3 Families of Indians who had left Athabasca the same day that we did, they did not bring me a single Fowl, they said they marched so hard, that they could not kill enough of Provision for their Families. By a Meridian line I found the Variation of the Compass to be about 20 Degrees Easterly.'

Sunday, 14 June: 'came on very heavy Rain which inevitably must diminish the Ice in its present shattered Condition.'

Monday, 15 June: 'In the Morning the Bay still full of Ice And can't get at our Netts. about Noon the wind veered to the West'erd and uncovered our Netts, and cleared a Passage to the opposite Islands, we raise our Netts very much broken and not many Fish. Struck our Tents loaded and embarked at Sun Set made the Traverse in two Hours time, about 8 Miles N.E. b N. unloaded upon a small Island and gummed our Canoe at ½ past 11 P.M. being then as clear as to see to write this, we have not seen a star since the second Day we left Athabasca.'

Tuesday, 16 June: 'It blew very hard from the North'erd this Morning which prevented our Embarking, a vast quantity of floating Ice the Men and Indians caught some Trout with Hook and Line. Set a Nett which we took up again at 12 with three small Fish. I had an observation which gave 61°—28 North. The Wind moderated and we embarked about one our Course N.W. thro' Islands 10 Miles we took in much Water making several Traverse at 5 P.M. we landed and camped, set Netts and Hook and Lines. The Indians kill'd a Goose. N.B. Thundered this Day.'

Wednesday, 17 June: 'The Indians brought us back to a point where we made a very good Fishery, and they went a hunting as well as to look out a Passage amongst the Islands. At 3 P.M. they returned without meeting with any large Animals, they could not observe any Passage, but we expect that the wind which blows strong from the N.E. will make a Passage. They killed two Geese—about sun set the weather became much overcast, Thunder, Lightning and Rain.'

Thursday, 18 June: 'Two of our Hunters killed a Rain Deer and young one, they had seen two Indians with their Families. One of the Indians came to see us about 7 o'Clock, had nothing. they live upon Fish. they are waiting the Lake being clear to go to the other side of it.'

Friday, 19 June: 'the weather cloudy, wind changeable, pestered by muskettoes, tho' we are in a manner surrounded by Ice.'

It seems that the party had no protection against mosquitoes or black flies, except smoke from tobacco pipes and campfires. There are in Canada over 60 species of mosquitoes (though not Anopheles) and some 70 species of black flies (a vicious biter not to be confused with the plant louse seen on bean stalks, which goes by the same name). The massive attack which these insects mount upon northern travellers is a familiar theme in early journals.

Saturday, 20 June: 'Rained at Intervals till about 5 o'Clock, we loaded our Canoe and steered for the By Island W. 6 miles, when we came to the point of it at the foot, a Traverse which was full of Ice, we set our Netts and soon caught plenty of Fish . . . There are many Cranberries and Spring Onions of which we gathered plenty.'

Sunday, 21 June: 'Blew from the South'erd last night drove the Ice to the North'erd . . . at 5 the Ice was almost all drove past to the Northerd, we embarked, making our way thro' much broken Ice steering W. 15 miles on the outside of the Traverse, Island and the Ice; the latter seem to be very solid to the NE. . . . we espied some Rain Deer upon one of the neighbouring Islands, our Hunters went in pursuit of them and kill'd 5 large and 2 small ones, which was not difficult Matter, the poor Creatures having no Place to run to for Shelter. In consequence of this Capture the Island were named *Isle de Carribo*. I sat up all this Night reading to observe the suns setting and Rising he was under our Horizon 4 Hrs. 22 Min; Rose N.20 E. by Comass. Froze so hard during his absence that the Lake Crusted half a quarter of an Inch thick.'

Ice on Midsummer Night: it underlines the precariousness of warmth in these high latitudes. Mackenzie, at this point, was approaching if not already within the region of permafrost, where below the depth of a few feet the soil is permanently frozen.

Monday, 22 June: 'I had an Observation at Noon which gave me 61°53″ North, the variation of the Compass about 2 pts. Mr Leroux's People hid 2 Bags Pemican in the Island for their return which occasioned it to be named *Is la Cach*.'

Tuesday, 23 June: 'thro' Islands we often carried Sail, the Wind having veered a little to the Eastard, this Course 16 Miles. Here we landed at half past 2 P.M. at 3 lodges of Red-knife Indians some of those that had given parole to Mr Leroux. They informed us that there were as many more lodges of their Friends not far off, one of them went immediately, they told us this was all we would see at present. that the Slave and Beaver Indians as well as others of their Tribe will be here by the time that the Swans cast their Feathers. It rained in Torrent upon us this afternoon.'

The 'parole' given to Leroux was, of course, a promise to trade furs only with him. In this region, remote from competition, it would not as yet be difficult to keep one's word. The few glimpses we have of Leroux, 'one of the Company's clerks', suggest that he was an old hand who had served under Pond and was familiar with the country, the Indians and the trade. He was evidently a great help to Mackenzie at this juncture.

Wednesday, 24 June: 'Traded above 8 packs good Beaver and Muslin with those People (in two hours time) . . . In the afternoon I called the Indians together and informed them that I intended to leave them tomorrow Morning but that Mr Leroux would remain here till the Indians that they spoke [of] should arrive, and in case they would bring Skins enough to fill his Canoe. that he would send the Frenchmen for more foods in order that he might winter here and build a Fort, which would be continued to them as long as they would deserve it.'

Thursday, 25 June: 'parted with Mr Leroux at 3 this Morning our Canoe very deeply laden having embarked some P[iece]s that had come in the other Canoe till here, Mr Leroux got his men & Indians to salute us with several Vollies to which we returned a few Shot . . . In the Traverse I found 6 Fathoms Water, a Sand Bottom. The Land on this Side has quite a different appearance from that from where we entered the lake till here. The latter is but one continued View of Mountains & Islands & Solid Rock covered here and there with Moss, Shrubs & Trees, the latter quite stinted in their Growth for want of Soil to nourish them; notwithstanding this barren appearance you can hardly land upon these Rocks but you will meet with Gooseberries—Cramberries whoilee Berries Brow Berries Juniper Berries, Rasberries, what the men call *Grains a Perdres* Grain a Saccacomir and what the Indians call *Pythagominan* something like a Rasberry but the last grows upon a small stalk $1\frac{1}{2}$ ft. high in wet Mossy Places all those are in great plenty tho' they do not all grow in one and the same Place . . . The Hunters kill'd 2 Swan and a Beaver. We landed at 8 oClk unloaded & gummed our Canoe as usual: &c.'

Friday, 26 June: 'we landed and continued our Rout (5 oClk) Steering S.E. for 10 Miles across 2 deep Bays. then S.S.E. Islands in Sight to the Eastward, travers'd another Bay 3 Miles, then S. 1 mile to a point which we named the detour, S.S.W. 4½ Miles a heavy Swol of the Lake. had an observation here 61°. 40 North Lat: S.W. 4 miles, W.S.W. among Islands . . . N.B. My Steersman had a misunderstanding with his Lady last Night & arranged her to remain at the Campmt. but his Cousin (her Furreaux) got her on board & the Husband said nothing to the contrary.'

Mackenzie makes only casual and occasional reference to the Indian women who accompanied his expedition. They were, however, quite indispensable, not least for their skill in making moccasins, of which an active man could on rocky terrain wear out a pair in one day. The skill, fortitude and resource of these women comes out clearly in Samuel Hearne's account of finding, in January, 1772, a young squaw living alone in a hut she had built. Escaping from a band that had taken her prisoner and unable to find the way to her own country, she had lived for seven months by snaring birds and small animals, had struck fire from two stones, had made herself a suit of rabbit skins and was busy fabricating a fish net from willow bark.

Saturday, 27 June: 'By 3 this morning we were under way after a very restless Night being tormented with Musquittoes . . . our guides quite at a loss they do not know what course to take he says its 8 winters since he has been here, that this Bay is much like the Entrance of the River in consequence we steered down the Bay about W.S.W. Course till we got in amongst Fields of Broken Ice still we could not see the Bottom of the Bay nor could we proceed. The Fog coming on made it very difficult for us to get to an Island S.W. of us, it was near dark when we landed upon it and camped.'

Sunday, 28 June: 'At a quarter past 3 this Morning we were on the Water . . . having a strong aft wind we lost sight of the Indians nor could we put ashore to wait for them without running the Risk of wrecking our Canoe till we came to the bottom of the Bay and ran our Canoe in amongst Bushes . . . did not Camp till Sunset. the English Chief was in a great Passion with the Red Knif wanted to shoot him for having undertaken to guide us in a Road he did not know, indeed none of us are well pleased with him, but we don't think with the English Chief that he merits such severe punishm't. besides he gave us some hopes that we are close by the River, that he recollects to have passed from the River thro' the wood to the Place that we landed at.'

Monday, 29 June: 'Embarked at 4 oClk this Morning steering along the S.W. Side of the Bay at ½ past 5 we came to the extremity of the point which we doubled & found it to be the Passage we were in search of, occasioned by a very long Island which separated this from the Main Channel of the River.'

He was at last in the current of the great northern river and during these days of frustration, as he sought an outlet from the lake, the elements of his enterprise had all taken the shape that would characterize them throughout. His basic problem was one of logistics, specifically of transportation. How to move the necessary weight of supplies over a water route punctuated by rapids, interrupted by gruelling portages, obstructed by driftwood, sandbars and ice packs: this was the ceaseless preoccupation.

In the mighty flow of the great river, they were now making good progress. At first the stream was wide and shallow, with many islands, but as they proceeded it contracted into a single swift current. On Wednesday, 1 July, they 'loaded and push'd off at a quarter before 4 A.M. . . . at one oClock there came on Thunder, Lightening, Wind and Rain, which ceased in about $\frac{1}{2}$ an Hour and left us wet to the Skin as we did not land. Great Quantities of Ice along the Banks of the River. Landed upon a small Island where there were the Poles of 4 Lodges, which we concluded to have been Crees, upon their War Excursions by appearance 6 or 7 years since. This Course for 15 Miles then W. where the River of the Mountain falls in from the Southerd. It appears to be a large River upwards of $\frac{1}{2}$ Mile over, at the Entry. About 6 miles further a small River from the same Direction, this Course 24 Miles we landed opposite to an Island the Mountains to the Southerd in S[igh]t. as our Canoe is very deep laden and that we are in daily Expectations of coming to the Rapids, which we have been made to dread, we hid 2 Bags of pemican in the opposite Island which I expect may be of Service to us in time to come, tho' our Indians are of a difft. opinion, they having no Expectations of coming back here, this Season, of course it will be lost Close by are two Indian Campments of last Years by their way of cutting the Wood they must have had no Iron Works. The Currt. was very strong all Day the Indians killed 2 Swans.'

During that day they covered at least one hundred miles. His 'River of the Mountain' is today known as the Liard, its smaller neighbour is the Martin River. Mackenzie was travelling north-west and must have been at this stage very hopeful of finding a way through the mountains to the Pacific.

On Thursday, 2 July, however, the Rockies, which had previously been seen afar off, were apparent as a barrier, 'the Tops of them hid in the Clouds'. They were close enough to see stones gleaming in the sun, white as talc, which the Indians called 'Maneloe Aseniah' or spirit stones. And, significantly, the course of the river changed to almost due north.

On Friday, 3 July, Mackenzie with two voyageurs and several Indians climbed a high hill to get a view of the country. They reached the summit after an hour and a quarter of hard walking but found their prospect limited by their encirclement among similar hills; 'between the Hills are Nos. of small Lakes upon which we could perceive many Swans, the Country appeared very thinly wooded, a few Trees of the Pine and Birch, and very small in Size, we were obliged to shorten our Stay here on account of the Swarms of Muskettoes that attacked us and were the only Inhabitants of the Place.' On Saturday, 4 July, the expedition made excellent time, setting off at 5 a.m. and at 8 p.m. pitching tents upon an island, after a run of over a hundred miles. The hours of darkness were now, at this high latitude and time of year, very brief. On Sunday, 5 July, the sun set at 55 minutes past 9, by Mackenzie's watch, and rose before 2 a.m. He was now anxious to get in touch with natives able to tell him what lay ahead downriver. Seeing the smoke of campfires, he made for the shore and saw Indians running about in great confusion, some taking to the woods, others to their canoes. English Chief and his young men finally succeeded in persuading some who understood the Chipewyan languages to come down to where the tents had just been pitched. They came 'with great Reluctance, and not without evident Signs of Fear, but the Reception they met with partly removed their Terror. and they recalled the rest of their People from their hiding Places. there are 5 Families of them in all, 26 or 30 Persons, and of two difft. tribes, Slave and Dog Rib Indian, we made them smoak, tho' it was evident they did not know the use of Tobacco, we like-wise gave them some Grog to drink, but I believe they accepted of those Civilities more through Fear than Inclina-tion by the Distribution of Knives, Beads, Awls, Rings, Gartering, Fire Steels, Flints and a couple of Axes, they became more familiar than we expected, for we could not keep them out of our Tents, tho' I did not observe that they tryed to steal anything from us.'

What Mackenzie most wanted, useful information about the river ahead, was not forthcoming. He was told they would be several winters getting to the sea and would all be old men by the time they returned, that besides 'many Monsters' there were two impassable falls or rapids. Though Mackenzie was unmoved by all this, English Chief and his young men, already sick and tired of the voyage, urged an immediate return and added that they understood game to become more and more scarce lower down, so that apart from all other perils certain starvation lay ahead. In situa-tions of this kind, Mackenzie was unfailingly resourceful, persuasive and triumphant. 'I with much ado dissuaded them out of their Reasonings.' He moreover induced, though with great difficulty, one of the local Indians to accompany them. He embarked only under suasion and before he left per-formed a parting ceremony of which the meaning could only be conjectured: 'he cut a lock of his Hair separated it into 3 Parts one of which he fastened to the hair of the Crown of his Wifes head, blowing on it three times as hard as he could & repeating some words, the other two he fastened with the same Ceremony on the heads of his two children.'

Mackenzie left on record, at some length, the manners and appearance of these Slave and Dog Rib Indians. Men and women danced in a ring, a bone dagger or piece of stick in one upraised hand, the other hand moving horizontally in time to their singing. Leaping and posturing, 'at every pause they make the Men give a howl in Imitation of the Wolf, or some other Animal & those that hold out the longest at this strong exercise seem to pass for the best Performers; the Women hang their Arms as if without the Power of Motion. They are all an ugly meagre ill made People particularly about the Legs which are very clumsy & full of Scabs by their frequent roasting them to the Fire. Many of them appear'd very sickly owing as I imagine to their Dirty way of living. They are of the Middle Stature & as far as could be discerned thro' Dust & Grease that cover their whole Body fairer than the generality of Indians, who inhabit warmer climes.' Commenting on the nakedness of the men, Mackenzie adds drily, 'their want of Modesty & their having no Sense of their Nakedness but from the Cold would make a Person think that they were descended from Adam, and probably had he been created at the Arctic Circles he would not have had occasion for Eve, the Serpent, nor the Tree of Knowledge to have given him a Sense of his Nakedness'.

On Monday, 6 July, the expedition made about 110 miles. The next day they entered with misgivings one of the rapids about which the Indians had given horrid warnings but 'did not find the Current stronger than elsewhere'. An attempt to secure another guide from one of the Indian encampments was unsuccessful, as 'he took the first Opp'ty to slip off with himself, and did not see him afterwards'. They were warned of the Eskimo—'very wicked and will kill us all'. On 8 and 9 July, there was more trouble over guides, but, continuing downstream, Mackenzie found Indians of another tribe who furnished a more reliable conductor, who 'spoke much in derision of the last Indians who we had seen, that they were all like old Women & great Liars &c, which coincides with the opinion I had already entertained of them'. The new guide assured Mackenzie they would reach the sea after sleeping ten more nights. A small party of Indians of a tribe known as Quarrellers were delighted to receive beads, especially blue ones.

On Friday, 10 July, they found that the river widened and ran in many channels among islands. They had in fact entered the delta of the Mackenzie. From this point on it is difficult to interpret mileages and references to places in the Journal. The slight air of confusion is understandable. They were now in a region of sandspits and mud banks, of ice and earth intermixed and of doubtful channels. The snow-clad Rockies were visible, 'running to the Northward as far as we could see'. Mackenzie tried for an observation to determine his latitude and at noon succeeded. He obtained 67° 47', 'which is further North than I expected, according to the Course I kept, but the difference is partly owing to the Variation of the Compass which is more Easterly than that I thought. I am much at a loss here how to act being certain that my going further in this Direction will not answer the Purpose of which the Voyage was intended, as it is evident these Waters must empty themselves into the Northern Ocean.' His Indians became so discouraged at this juncture that he promised to continue only seven more days, 'and that if I did not come to the sea in that time that I should return, and my scarcity of Provisions will make me fulfil this promise, whether I will or not'.

On Saturday, 11 July, Mackenzie notes, 'I sat up last Night to observe at what time the Sun would set, but found that he did not set at all at half past 12 I called upon one of the Men to see what he never saw before.'

They were now in Eskimo country and found huts of drift-wood, branches and dried grass. Sledge runners, pieces of whalebone and fish floats lay scattered about. Mackenzie was eager to get information about the country, but no Eskimo were encountered. On Sunday, 12 July, they found more houses, and equipment including 'a square Stone Kettle, could contain about 2 Galls., its very surprising how they could have dug it out, the Bottom is flat'. Seeing nothing but ice ahead, they camped and Mackenzie decided that this was as far as they could go. Climbing to the highest point of the island they had reached, 'we could see the Ice in a whole Body extending from the S.W. by Compass to the Eastward as far as we could see—To the Southward we could just perceive a Chain of Mountains extending farther to the North than the Edge of the Ice distant upwards of 20 leagues to the Eastward are great many Islands.' It must by now have been apparent that in a negative sense the object of his descent of the great river was accomplished. It led not to the Pacific but to the Arctic and there was no 'north-west passage' at a higher latitude than he had reached because even in midsummer the ice appeared impassable.

At this point the indomitable spirit of the voyageurs, as contrasted to the Indians, manifested itself. 'My Men express much sorrow that they are obliged to return without seeing the Sea, in which I believe them sincere for we marched exceed'g hard coming down the River, and I never heard them grumble; but on the contrary in good Spirits, and in hopes every day that the next would bring them to the *Mer d'Ouest*, and declare themselves now and at any time ready to go with me wherever I choose to lead them.'

On Monday, 13 July, the water rose in the night, and the significance was not realized. The next day they saw creatures which Mackenzie identified as a species of white whale and they pursued them but were foiled by fog. Providentially, for as the *Voyages* interpolates here: 'It was, indeed a very wild and unreflecting enterprise, and it was a very fortunate circumstance that we failed in our attempt to overtake them, as a stroke from the tail of one of these enormous fish would have dashed the canoe to pieces.' This spectacle of a crew of voyageurs in a birch-bark canoe chasing whales amid Arctic icefields remains a splendid oddity in the historical record of Canada. Later in the day, the whole party paddled out to inspect the ice but encountered a rising swell and were almost swamped. Mackenzie decided to run no more such risks but simply to spend the next two or three days looking for Eskimo among the islands. He gave the name Whale Island to the spot where he was encamped.

There was reason for some initial uncertainty as to whether they had reached the Arctic because the delta is shallow and the water around Whale Island is fresh and full of sediment. The tidal range does not exceed one or two feet but a northwest wind will raise the level four or five feet. It is a region of permafrost and ground ice, yet trees, often of the low form known as Krummholz, come right down the valley. In the delta are trunks with two or three hundred annual rings. The lower valley shelters some moose and there are always fish and rabbits.

Here was the end of the northward voyage. 'This Morning I fixed a Post close by our Campmt. on which I engraved the latitude of the Place. My own Name & the Number of Men with me & the time we had been here.' As he put up his marker, it was late afternoon or evening in Paris and the Bastille had fallen. We cannot say which was the more significantly symbolic action but it may well turn out, in the long perspective of history, that this voyage of Mackenzie's which established a British (and later Canadian) claim to the Arctic seaboard flanking the mouth of the river, was the more portentous of the two events.

On Wednesday, 15 July, the water rose again and it was

recognized that this must be a tidal movement and not merely an effect of the wind. The next day there was a renewed search for Eskimo, 'but all to no purpose, Our Conductor says they are gone to where the[y] fish for whales, & kill Rein Deer opposite to his Land, & that he & his Relations sees them there every Year that the Water is very deep there, & that we shall see none of them, without it be at a small River that falls into the grand River from the East-ward, & a good way from here, by the Way that he wanted us to come down, as we give up hopes of seeing any of the Natives here abouts we made for the River & stemm'd the Currt. at 2 oClk P.M. the water was quite shallow every where we passed cou'd always find bottom with a Paddle.' Although Mackenzie does not say specifically that he is turn-ing back, and although he is clearly still in hopeful search of Eskimo, it is at this point that he begins his return journey.

On Friday, 17 July, they passed deserted encampments and Mackenzie examined the construction of a small canoe and of several sledges, with the curious, loving eye of a man who daily trusts his life to a few thin wooden slats covered with frail bark. The next day they killed two reindeer and found berries in abundance. 'Our Pemmican has been mouldey this long time past, but in our Situation we must eat it & not loose a particle of it.' These reindeer (caribou) were in fact the only large animals they had seen since leav-ing Great Slave Lake, and must have been doubly welcome.

On Sunday, 19 July, their guide had gone when they woke, leaving behind the skin Mackenzie had given him to cover himself. Mackenzie was surprised at his honesty and concerned that in such cold weather he should possess only his shirt. The Indians thought he was afraid of being carried off as a slave and frightened when he saw them kill the reindeer with such ease. It is not surprising that guides were elusive, unreliable and recalcitrant. They had no stake in the expedition and got small returns for taking daily risks of an incalculable kind.

Returning upstream, it seems to have taken two days to cover the equivalent of one day's journey downstream. Still no Eskimo, though on Wednesday, 22 July, they learned from wayside Indians that 'The Eskmeaux saw large Canoes full of White Men to the Westward 8 or 10 Winters since, from whom they got Iron of which they exchang'd part with them for Leather. where the big Canoes came to, they call *Belan howlay Tock*. (White Mens lake).' Most likely these men in ships were Russians. It has been conjectured that the meeting place was in the vicinity of Point Barrow.

Food was now plentiful. On Thursday, 23 July, Mackenzie notes, 'we did not touch our Provision these 6 Days past in which time we have eat 2 Rein Deer, 4 Swans, 45 Geese, 1 Brant & a great many Fish among 10 Men 4 Women & a Boy, I always found North Men bless'd with good appetites. but nothing equal to what ours are, & has been since we enter'd the River, I would have thot. it gluttoness in my Men, did I not find that my own Appetite has augmented in proportion to theirs.'

The next day Mackenzie found among the stones bits of what appeared to be yellow wax, which he identified as petroleum. As he was prospecting not for oil but for furs, it was of no great interest.

On Saturday, 25 July, a violent storm 'Broke the Ridge Pole of my Tent in the Middle where it was sound & 9½ Ins in Circumference we were obliged to throw ourselves flat upon the Ground to escape being hurt by Stones that were hurled about by the Air like Sand.'

The next day they encountered a Dog Rib Indian, living here in exile. English Chief understood him very easily and he had something to say of great concern to Mackenzie: 'he informed us that he understood from the People with whom he now lives (Hare Indians) that there is another large River on the other Side of the Mountains to the S.W. which falls into the *Belhowlay Toe* in comparison to which this is but a small River that the Natives are Big and very wicked, kill Common Men with their Eyes, that they make Canoes larger than Ours, that those at the Entry kill a kind of a large Beaver the Skin of which is almost Red, that there has been by Canoes [those who] say Ships there often, he knows of no Communication by water to the above River, those of the Natives who saw it went over the Mountains on Foot.' In all likelihood, the river referred to is the Yukon and the ships Russian. On Monday, 27 July, Mackenzie hears more about the river to the west and of a white men's fort, which he takes to be the Russian post of 'Unalaschka'. He was, however, now becoming increasingly exasperated over his inability to get new and reliable information. He was hearing old wives' tales about natives on the far side of the range, some who kill common men by looking at them, others who have wings though they do not fly. He was also of the opinion that his interpreter who was 'now & long since tired of the Voyage' was concealing information from him. The Indians they met were afraid of being carried off. Mackenzie traded a few beaver skins, distributed small gifts, was obliged to shoot a dog that stole their provisions, and noted with repulsion that some of the women, 'as ugly and disagreeable Beings as can be', were being bribed to spend the night. They were now in sight of smoke from ever-burning lignite. Next day they reached the area of the Ramparts and were soaked in a sudden storm that blew down their tents and nearly carried away the canoe. The weather was extremely variable and on Wednesday, 29 July, Mackenzie writes, 'Yesterday the Heat was insupportable and today we can't put clothes enough on to keep us warm.' The next day, 'English Chief had a dispute with one of his young Men, he discovered that he was too intimate with his young Wife, and that she was to run away with him when they would get to their own Country. This is all I could learn of their Discourse.'

Friday 31 July was a typical day on the return voyage. It had rained all night but by mid-afternoon the wind died away and it became warm; later in the day the east wind chilled them. There were 'Whurtle Berries, Rasberries, &c' in abundance along the shore but sandbanks made it difficult to land. In other places, the crumbling bank of black earth showed solid ice a foot below the surface of the water. They killed seven geese and Mackenzie notes with satisfaction, 'Tonight we begin upon our Corn, we ate only 3 Days upon our Provision since we began to mount the Curt.' He would like to have taken the side opposite to the one he came down on 'to see if there are any Rivers of consequence coming in from the westward' but there were too many sandbanks and too strong a current, so he traversed back to the old side where the eddies were more frequent, making for easier paddling and a larger catch of fish. Food and fairly rapid headway were the essentials of a successful operation.

The next day they were within a few miles of the spot where Great Bear River debouches into the Mackenzie and had by this time left the latitudes of the midnight sun. 'Tonight is the first Time it has been dark enough to see a Star since we left Athabasca.' The brevity of Summer at this latitude was illustrated the day following when a party that went out to look for Indians returned with a beaver they had killed: 'its Fur begin to get long, which is a sure sign of the approach of the Fall.' There was another sign of seasonal change. 'This being the Time that the Rein Deer leaves the

Plains to come to the wood as the Musquittoes time is almost over, makes me apprehensive that we will not find a single Indian on the River Side as they will be in or abt. the Mountains setting Snares to catch Careboeuff.'

Day after day the expedition worked its way back against the current. The weather was trying in the rapidity of its change. 'it is so cold today,' Mackenzie notes on Wednesday, 5 August, 'that our marchg. don't keep us warm with all our Cloaths on—at Noon Yesterday we found our Shirt too heavy.' They were very much fatigued with tracking along stony banks. 'Women are continually employ'd making Shoes, as a pair does not last us above one Day.' From time to time welcome relief came from 'a strong aft wind which with the help of our Paddles drove us on at a good rate'. In spite of the weather and frequent landings to look for Indians or hunt for food, he was making thirty miles a day.

On Monday, 10 August, the mountains on the south-west side of the river looked so accessible that Mackenzie set off with one of the young Indians to make an ascent. He was, of course, determined to find out what lay on the other side. After three hours' walking, they appeared to be no nearer. His companion was eager to return, as his shoes and leggings were torn to pieces. Mackenzie's intrepid spirit was again evident. 'I persisted in proceeding & that we wou'd pass the Night in the Mountains & return in the Morning, as we approach'd them the grd became quite Marshy & we waded in Water & Grass up to the Middle till we came within a Mile of the Foot of the Mountains, where I fell in up to the Arm Pits & with some difficulty extricated myself. I found it impossible to proceed in a Stt. Line & the Marsh extended as far as I could see, so that I did not attempt to make the Circuit, so therefore thought it most prudent to make the best of my Way back to my Canoe (tho' it was Night when

I arriv'd after 12 oClk very much fatigued.)' This ability to push himself and others to the limit in the single-minded pursuit of an objective, yet never to lose control of things or fail to provide for a return to base—this is in miniscule the whole of Mackenzie's strategy.

On Thursday, 13 August, they reached the island where their pemmican was cached and found it intact 'and is very acceptable to us, as it will enable us to get out of the River without losing much time to hunt'. Indians were seen and Mackenzie was, as usual, eager to communicate with them. His own Indians seemed, to his great annoyance, to be more concerned with furs and hunting equipment left on the beach as their owners took to the woods to avoid the party. At this point his displeasure with English Chief boiled over, who in turn became furious. 'I waited such an opportunity to tell him his Behaviour to me for some time past, told him that I had more Reason to be angry than he, that I had come a great way at a great Expence to no Purpose, and that I thot. he hid from me part of what the Natives told him respecting the Country &c. for fear that he should have to follow me, and that his Reason for not killing was his Jealousy, which likewise kept him from looking for the Natives, as he ought, and that we never had given him any Reason for such Suspicion. He got into a most violent Passion, and said, we spoke ill, that he was not jealous, that he had not concealed any thing from us, and that till now there were no Animals and that he would not accompany us any further tho' he was without Ammunition, he cou'd live the same as the Slaves, and that he would remain among them &c. &c. as soon as he was done his Harrangue he began to cry bitterly, and his Relations help'd him, they said they cried dead Friend, I did not interrupt them in their Grief for two Hours, as I could not well [do] without them, I was obliged to use every method to make the

English Chief change his Mind, at last he consented with a great Reluctance, and we embark'd.' The irreconcilable difference between Mackenzie and his guides is here apparent. His mind was filled with plans that included even bringing vessels round Cape Horn. He was prepared to drive himself through all obstacles and across all barriers. The Indians, with reason, wanted a limited commitment to travelling and an assured return to their timeless, unlocated way of life. That evening Mackenzie took a quiet walk along the bank of the river, white with salt where the receding waters had dried away. He was himself a good deal calmer now. 'I invited the English Chief to sup with me, I gave him a Dram or two and were as good friends as ever. he told me that it was the Custom of the Chipewean Chiefs to go to War after the Crees, and that next Spring he should go for certain, that he would remain and do as he used to do for the French people till that time, gave him a little Grog to carry to his Tent to drown his Chagrine, the Indians killed 3 Geese today, fair weather.' It was evidently a bad day for Mackenzie, but all's well that ends well.

On Sunday, 16 August, Mackenzie remarks, 'the Current is not strong, we go up it nearly as fast as in dead water'. They were paddling about thirty miles a day and must have made fifty miles on Monday, 17 August. But the strain told. 'My foreman who lead the March had some Words with one of my Steersmen for hard marching, that he did not give them time to eat or smoak &c. they wanted to land to see who was the best Man, but it was not deemed necessary to comply with their Request, I interfered and all was over, this is the first and only dispute of the kind that we have had since we commenced our Voyage. One of the young Indians lost a gun belonging to one of the Men, it fell overboard out of his Canoe.'

They were nearly out of provisions. The paddles were worn and new ones had to be made. An observation on Tuesday, 18 August, gave 61° 33′ North latitude and on the morning of Saturday, 22 August, under half sail, they came to the entrance of Great Slave Lake. T. H. McDonald, who in 1965 followed the party's route in a canoe, remarks that it took Mackenzie thirty-two days to make about 910 miles, returning to Great Slave Lake, in comparison with thirteen days spent covering the same distance with the current. Allowing for time lost in hunting or exploring and when stormbound, we find that he averaged one hundred miles a day going downstream and better than thirty upstream. 'This is a phenomenal record.'

As before, the great lake proved treacherous. Mackenzie determined to skirt the coast, partly for fish and partly in hope of meeting Leroux. They were driving on under half sail when the yard broke; they took in water 'and had our Mast given way in all probability we should have filled and sunk, we went on with great Danger, being along a flat leeshore, not able to land till 3 o'Clock p.m. 2 men continually Bailing out the water which we took in on every Side, doubled a Point which screened us from the Wind and Swell. Camped for the Night, and to wait for our Indians, set Nets, make a Yard and Mast, Gummed our Canoe.'

On Monday, 24 August, they met Leroux who, with his family, was on a hunting party. He had been trading furs with great success since his chief's departure and he had surplus stores with him, most welcome to Mackenzie's party who for some time had been living on the land. Mackenzie added some rum to cheer them up after their long struggle against the current. English Chief's party had narrowly escaped drowning when their canoes broke and were 'quite exhausted with fatigue'. On Saturday, 29 August, the Indians told Mackenzie they were determined not to follow him any more having already run so many risks and being afraid of getting drowned. The next day they reached a house Leroux had built on the north shore of the lake and Mackenzie records how 'accordg. to promise I gave my Indians a good Equipment of Iron work, Ammunition Tobacco &c. &c. as a recompense for the misery they underwent along with me.'

On Monday, 31 August, Mackenzie continued, leaving Leroux and English Chief behind to collect furs. The trade was, after all, his main concern and he pleased himself with the thought that during the winter every skin the Athabasca country could produce would be earmarked for his own company. The few trade goods he had remaining were left with Leroux and more promised. He left at 5 a.m., not having gone to bed all night. He had eighty pounds of pemmican from Leroux and, though some Indian children had shot an arrow through the canoe below water mark, the leak was discovered and repaired by noon. He was now feeling his way along the north shore of the lake, which is interrupted by the enormous wedge of Yellowknife Bay, and trying to reach the mouth of Slave River on the opposite side of the lake. It took him at least four days to do so. His entries are brief and not entirely clear except as to the discomfort and peril of his crossing. In a traverse of twelve miles they 'took a good deal of Water', then a favourable wind makes possible a traverse of twenty-four miles and Mackenzie is cheered— 'Our takg this Traverse shortened our Road 3 Leagues, we did not expect to have got clear of the lake in such a situation.' After this it 'Blew exceeding hard all Night, we embarked at 4 AM and took us 3 hours to go 5 Miles without stopping, notwithstanding we were screened from the Swall by a large Bank.'

Bad weather persisted as they worked upstream on the

Slave River toward their destination, Lake Athabasca. A strong North wind and torrential rain, through which they could see numerous flocks of wildfowl already flying south. Monday, 7 September, was a typical day: 'Embarked at half past 5 this Morning, a hard Wind, frequent showers of small Rain, at 3 oClk PM ran our Canoe upon a Stump, and before we could land, she filled with Water, we took 2 Hours to repair her, we Camped at 7 oClk PM.' They were now arrived at the long series of portages on the Slave. On Wednesday, 9 September, the canoe broke on the men's shoulders and the guide mended her while the others carried the baggage. The next day they encountered a small party of Crees coming back from a raid and suffering from sickness and starvation. With one of the sick Mackenzie dealt in his customarily masterful way. The man believed that his sickness was the result of witchcraft, that his enemies 'had thrown medicine at him' and he despaired of recovery. Mackenzie could only administer 'Turlington's balsam mixed in water' but assured him of a cure if he would never again go to war against defenceless people. The patient promised, recovered, 'was true to his engagements, and on all occasions manifested his gratitude to me'. The whole story appears in the *Voyages*; in the *Journal* there is only the vivid sentence, 'I gave Medicine to the Sick, and a little Ammunition to the healthy which they were much in Need of, having lived by their Bows and Arrows this 6 months, they have suffered very much.'

Autumn was now upon the north country; signs had been apparent during the latter part of their journey. On Friday, 11 September, Mackenzie records, 'Embarked at half past 4 AM, froze hard last Night, cold weather throughout the Day, Appearance of Snow.' The next day (though, in his eagerness to be done with the voyage, he runs the two entries together), 'the Wind veered to the Westward, and as strong as we could bear it with high Sail, which wafted us to Fort Chipewean by 3 oClk PM here we found Mr McLeod with 5 Men busy building a new House 102 Days since we had left this Place.'

So ends Mackenzie's first voyage and the *Journal* appears to end also. But after one blank page, three more pages of script appear, in which Mackenzie offers the reader 'A few remarks to elucidate my tracks from Athabasca latitude 58. 38 North and longitude 110½ West from Greenwich to the North Sea [Arctic] and western ocean.' A summary of his second voyage follows and he concludes, 'I have not the least doubt of this great River being navigable with canoes and boats to its mouth. I have mentioned above the cause of my not putting this to the proof. It abounds in Salmon and other fish, is well inhabited they cloathe themselves in fur and skins and live by fishing and hunting.'

What river he in fact refers to, as navigable the whole way down to the Pacific Ocean, we shall discover in due course. Here, as his first great voyage ends, it is enough to see how eager he is for the reader to be aware that he, Mackenzie, did reach salt water in the west and found the heart's desire of all fur traders—a vast new territory, well inhabited, rich in furs, plentiful in fish and game, traversed by a great navigable river flowing into the temperate waters of a known and accessible ocean. But all this, as he now finds McLeod with five men busy building a new house for the winter, is in the distant future. He has in the meantime some preparations to make of a far reaching kind which will necessitate a return to Britain and he is still a fur trader with responsibilities to his company and a report to make. He is aware now, as always, that his partners will be much concerned about the furs that Athabasca has yielded and very little, if at all, interested in his penetration of the remote north, the land of Eskimo and whales and drifting ice.

He found at Fort Chipewyan that Roderick had actively pursued the collecting of furs and had been down to report at company headquarters in Grand Portage. In the spring, Alexander went down to the regular gathering of the partners. Their indifference to his recent achievement and future plans did not surprise him. A letter to the faithful Roderick says summarily, 'My expedition was hardly spoken of, but that is what I expected.' He was nevertheless a valued member of the North West Company. The Athabasca country yielded by far the best returns of all the company's districts. An arrangement was reached whereby the company would consist of ten partners. Mackenzie was to hold for his part, a one-tenth interest in the concern.

It haunts the imagination, this voyage of Mackenzie's, because it offers a parable through which to interpret Canadian history. It is a record of intense physical effort, expended it would seem, in vain: there was no way out to the Pacific in that direction. The anxious daily entries in his journal; the ceaseless concern to establish latitude and longitude; the painful skirting of the ice covering Great Slave Lake; the quick enforced turnabout as food ran low; the absent Eskimo: it is a record of carefully manœuvred and exquisitely conserved effort in the face of a terrain so vast, so absurd, so all absorbing that effort, except to subsist, seems useless, and yet a terrain across which, driven by some vision or compulsion, men continually string out, from point to point, the means of communication. Beneath the apparent rationality, the commonsense search for commercial advantage, we sense a ruling passion which is not explicable in these terms, a desire like that of Tennyson's Ulysses, an acceleration of effort resembling that which sustains contemporary plans to conquer space. At one moment we see Mackenzie in the context of Cook and Vancouver, of Bruce and Mungo Park, of Australians or Americans attempting to cross a continent. And then he becomes unique and secret, a man whose obsession with a certain kind of success never rises into verbal expression. Our sense of identity with him is ineradicable, if only because the dream of ultimate achievement wraps itself so firmly in the disguise of a desire for commercial success and the daily painful progress, hour by hour, conceals the true scope of the endeavour.

Most national heroes are in some sense representative of the people who honour them. Mackenzie foreshadows a good deal of Canadian history. This is apparent even in his relation to his voyageurs.

Many readers of Xenophon's *Anabasis* will remember the sense of shock they experienced when, at the close of the narrative, the Greeks who have struggled with such painful endurance to reach the sea are now simply drafted into another army and go off to fight another war. The echo of this dismay is felt when Mackenzie's voyageurs are dismissed from his story and disappear. From other sources we learn that Jacques Beauchamp, who made the Pacific journey, was killed by Eskimo in 1802. Francois Beaulieux, another of the same crew, returned in the end to Quebec and settled down. At the age of seventy, thinking, perhaps, that he must prepare for another world, he was baptized, but he lived to be nearly a hundred. About the others almost nothing is known.

In the course of the narrative, Mackenzie's relation to his crew is always ambiguous. He relied on them, directed and encouraged them, looked to their supplies of food, went ahead if they were in danger and, in two very hazardous journeys, never lost a man or had a man suffer serious injury.

He had their loyalty; this is again and again demonstrated. Two, at least, of those who had been to the Arctic volunteered for the Pacific trip. If they rebelled at all, it was against the tyranny of the terrain, not against their leader. And yet, from the account, we scarcely know their names and they barely, throughout the journeys, emerge as individuals. One is tempted, in view of the present strained relations between French-Canadians and 'Anglais' in Canada, to see in Mackenzie the assumption of superiority and indifference to French interests of which English-Canadians are so often accused. The truth is more complex and shows itself even in the relation between Mackenzie and Alexander Mackay, the Scotsman who took part in the Pacific voyage. It is clear that he was valuable to Mackenzie but we have very little sense of his presence. At one point in the narrative, however, when morale was so low that, for the first and only time, the party was in danger of splitting up, Mackenzie inserts, as an afterthought, a footnote concerning Mackay: 'It is but common justice to him, to mention in this place that I had every reason to be satisfied with his conduct.' Poor Mackay was killed in 1811 in the famous *Tonquin* disaster which took place near Nootka. An Indian massacre followed by an explosion took the lives of all on board; it is said that Mackay, struck by a war club, was the first to fall. The massacre was in consequence of atrocious behaviour on the part of the captain, a violent contrast to Mackenzie's studied moderation.

The root of Mackenzie's relation with his men goes very deep. It reaches into the fundamental concept of loyalty which governed the Montreal fur trade; an Indian who took his furs to a New York trader was considered to have forfeited the trust put in him, to have been disloyal. For Mackenzie this concept would be strengthened by the clan loyalties which had surrounded his upbringing. The peculiarity of such loyalty is that it was to a great degree impersonal. A highland chief, at the time of the Forty-five, could threaten to burn the houses of clansmen who were slow to follow him. In later years, clansmen had little protection against a laird who, for the sake of enclosure and increased profits, decided to evict them. Mackenzie's voyageurs were nearly all French-Canadians, members of a colony which, after the fall of Quebec in 1759, had been deserted by its leaders, who returned to France. They were still feudal in their outlook, bound by tradition, uncritical, possessed of traditional skills and of an uncomplaining, laborious endurance beyond praise, at times almost beyond belief. Their concept of loyalty dovetailed into Mackenizie's with ease. But, again, there was no expectation of a personal bond, once the enterprise which had evoked loyalty to the leader was terminated. Great Canadian achievements in the building of railways, canals and dams have often repeated this pattern. The work is ended and those who achieved it are scattered and lost sight of. When the last spike of the C.P.R. was driven home, fulfilling, after a hundred years, Mackenzie's desire for a route to the ocean, Van Horne, the general manager, said simply, 'All I can say is that the work has been well done in every way.' But we do not remember the names of those who linked ocean to ocean as the names of de Lesseps and Brunel are remembered.

Another aspect of Mackenzie's voyages which seems representative of Canadian experience is his relation with the Indians he encountered. Until he reached the extremity of each journey, he was travelling wholly within the vast area where Athapascan languages were spoken. It is difficult to tie down Indian tribes with any accuracy, as there was considerable movement in search of food. The reader will find it useful, however, to locate the Athapascan speakers through whose lands Mackenzie passed on his first voyage roughly as follows: Chipewyan, east of Lake Athabasca; Beaver, west of the Lake; Slave, west of Great Slave Lake; Yellow Knife and Dog Rib, east and south of Great Bear Lake respectively; Hare, in the lower valley but not the delta of the Mackenzie. They were hunters and fishermen, living on caribou, whitefish, rabbits and birds. As we have seen, they had very little in the way of political or social structure.

The Indians who, as hunters, accompanied the expedition, like those who welcomed the sight of the strange canoes, or fled from them into the forest, or traded with the party, or threatened it, were all members of bands without a fixed centre of authority. Mackenzie never met a chief whose writ ran over the next mountain range. The Indians had none of the loyalty and steadfastness of the voyageurs. Nor could this be expected of them; their pattern of survival encouraged other qualities. Yet their knowledge of the country yielded up to Mackenzie in his journey, stage by stage, was vital to his success.

If the Indians were useful to Mackenzie, he was, of course, potentially of even more value to them. Only through the fur traders could they hope to acquire the cloth, the guns, the utensils and knives and files they found so convenient. Theirs was a static culture and could only be changed by contact with a culture possessed of the skills of reckoning. Mackenzie could calculate time, money, latitude and longitude, distances, weights and measures. His writing and figuring, his maps and accounts and journals, his rational planning and means of communication with Montreal, gave him powers no Indian chief possessed. The question he was asked, 'Do not you white men know everything in the world?' takes its full meaning when we stress the last phrase. The

Indian might be a better hunter and, indeed, a wiser man than the trader, but what went on in the world at large he did not know.

It is customary to speak of the fatal impact of European civilization upon native cultures. In western Canada, time is the essence of the disagreement between Indians and whites. The advance of calculation and mechanism has been too rapid for either natives or newcomers themselves to keep up with. Western Canadians are still preoccupied with Mackenzie's preoccupations: transport, trade, finance, the exploitation of natural resources.

Mackenzie's easy relations, as a trader and explorer, with Athapascan-speaking Indians are, of course, in contrast to the hostility and suspicion he encountered on the Pacific coast, where unscrupulous ships' captains, as much robbers as traders, were already known. And the ease of his dealings with the natives is in still sharper contrast with the long tale of savage struggle in the East, between French settlers and Iroquois. With this our story of Mackenzie has nothing to do. As luck would have it, he escaped the natural animosity the tribes felt for those who tried to conquer them, or settle their lands, or involve them in wars. And to his luck he added a faculty for managing men, in sharp contrast to many of his contemporaries, like the captain of the ill-fated *Tonquin*, whose violence toward the Indians led to an attack during which his crew were massacred and his ship destroyed. He was temperamentally averse to violence and had, in any case, no means of making more than a token show of force. To this day, Canadian diplomacy, even in the international field, is marked by deliberate caution, by a consistent desire for adjustment and compromise.

Mackenzie's life presents us with a paradigm that has again and again been repeated and is still a pronounced pattern of Canadian experience. The single individual, with inadequate information and equipment, and working in association with a corporate body that does not wholly understand or support his plan, may still be able, by practical means pursued with energy and single-mindedness, to accomplish something that will be of value to his country and perhaps prove, as time goes on, to have been of crucial and decisive importance at the moment of its accomplishment. And all this holding good in spite of errors, disappointments and lapses of judgment, on his own part and on the part of the society he works for. The construction of the Canadian Pacific Railway by John A. Macdonald, as prime minister, was an achievement of this order.

Mackenzie achieved what he did through the exercise of imaginative, yet infinitely hazardous and laborious, effort from day to day. His moral excellence is inseparable from achievement and shows itself only in that context and, indeed, appears to be produced by that context. He had no intellectual curiosity. He illustrates Canadian pragmatism and concern for financial success. He was always competitive. Taken out of the context of his two voyages, he hardens into the figure of a trader for whom the worlds of natural beauty, of art, of sensibility, of intellectual enquiry, of religion, hardly exist. And then we recall his well-known apologia: 'I had to encounter perils by land and perils by water; to watch the savage who was our guide, or to guard against those of his tribe who might meditate our destruction. I had also the passions and fears of others to control and subdue . . . The toil of our navigation was incessant, and oftentimes extreme.'

III

Interlude in England

DURING the winter of 1790–1, Mackenzie worked at the trade with his cousin, the former at Chipewyan, the latter at the mouth of Yellowknife River, where a new post was being established. Not for a moment, however, does Alexander show any sign of losing his determination to reach the Pacific. But first, on the principle of *reculer pour mieux sauter*, he decided to cross the Atlantic back to England, to learn more about the determining of geographical positions and to acquire better instruments. As regards determining latitude, he had done very well on his voyage to the Arctic. On 24 June, for example, his observation gave him 62° 24′ North Latitude and T. H. McDonald, who closely followed his route in 1965, estimates that he was at about 62° 30′. At most he was seven miles out. His belief that he needed more accurate methods was, nevertheless, correct. Concerning his Arctic expedition he was later to write. 'In this voyage I was not only without the necessary books and instruments, but also felt myself deficient in the sciences of astronomy and navigation. I did not hesitate therefore to undertake a winter's voyage in order to procure the one and acquire the other.'

The union of confidence, caution and courtesy in his character is nicely illustrated by two letters written back to Roderick as he was on his way through Grand Portage to Montreal. He hears that a certain Philip Turner has been sent from England by the Hudson's Bay Company to lead an expedition to the Pacific. This was a rival enterprise. Nevertheless Mackenzie wrote to Roderick to give Turner every accommodation and assistance. He then actually encountered Turner's party and wrote again, 'I find the intention of the expedition is discoveries only. I also find the party ill prepared for the undertaking.' What Turner did was to fix the longitude of Fort Chipewyan as 115° West. He had already experienced great difficulty in travelling, which was not remarkable in a newcomer to the country, and his observation of longitude at Fort Chipewyan put beside Cook's observation of 154° at the mouth of Cook's Inlet made it clear that the two points were separated by some 1,500 miles of mountainous country, heavily forested at lower levels and not known to possess a practicable system of waterways. He wisely made no attempt to assault this tangled wilderness upheaving itself on the western horizon.

Toward Turner Mackenzie's attitude was generous. He was willing to afford assistance in spite of his knowledge of Turner's objective, which was close to his own. Toward the memory of another Hudson's Bay man, Samuel Hearne, he seems to have been less charitable. Writing to Roderick in 1806, he says, 'I wish you would give instruction to collect from the English Chief and other Chippeweans the fullest account they possibly can give of Hearne's journey with them to the North sea where according to what I learn he never went.' He had perhaps been reading Hearne's posthumous volume, *A Journey from Prince of Wales's Fort . . . to the Northern Ocean*, published in 1795. Hearne had come to tidewater at the mouth of the Coppermine River in 1771 and was therefore the first overland explorer to reach the Arctic Ocean. His return journey took him across Great Slave Lake, anticipating Mackenzie in that respect, as well. His journeys, based on Hudson's Bay, brought out his incredible powers of endurance.

About Mackenzie's stay in England we know very little. He must have been eager, as he says, to acquire books and instruments useful in navigation and we may guess that he was alert to every report concerning the fur trade or concerning discoveries on the Pacific Coast.

In order to fix their positions, from day to day, the explorers of the north-west had to possess the instruments and the skills to determine both latitude and longitude. Latitude was the easier of the two to ascertain. The Pole Star, only slightly more than one degree off the true Pole, is always visible on a clear night and its altitude can readily be found by using a sextant or even a much cruder instrument. The sextant was not invented until about 1730, but Columbus, more than two centuries earlier, correctly reported the latitude of his landfall in the New World.

Even though he had crossed the ocean to England to learn more about astronomical navigation, and had made some effort to secure better equipment, Mackenzie was still distrustful of his own skill and his sextant was of an obsolete pattern. On midsummer's day, at noon, he tried to take an altitude but the angle was too great for the instrument.

His compass may have been graduated in degrees, though, following contemporary practice, he records his directions as 'East-South-East', 'South-East by East' and so forth. His care to record each change of direction and the distance covered is rather hard to explain because his observations fixed the latitude and longitude—time and weather permitting— whenever the expedition halted. Had he been map making, like David Thompson or Peter Fidler, this carefulness would be understandable. It seems probable that he wanted to leave a record that would make it easy for other North-Westers to follow his trail and it also is likely that he thought his dead reckoning, from point to point, more accurate than his astronomical observations, though this was not so in actual fact. He really had no means of knowing accurately how fast he was travelling in a canoe. For obvious reasons, he could not use a nautical log. He was obliged to make estimates based on the normal rate of paddling for his crew and the strength of the current, which, in turn, had to be estimated or guessed at.

In addition to sextant and compass, Mackenzie had a chronometer and a telescope, in order to establish his longitude. This was more difficult than finding one's latitude.

To put it very simply, to find his longitude a traveller needs to know two times, the time at the spot where he is standing, which can be obtained by observing the position of the sun, and the time at Greenwich Observatory, through which the prime meridian, by international agreement, runs. If one has a completely accurate timepiece set to Greenwich time, all is well. But it was exceedingly difficult, even in the eighteenth century, to construct a sufficiently accurate clock. As late as 1814, a reward of £10,000 was offered by the British Government for a method of obtaining longitudes within one degree of accuracy, or £20,000 for accuracy within half a degree. Half a degree of error, if a ship were sailing up the coast of what is now British Columbia, would result in an uncertainty of no more than some thirty-five miles. This would be wonderfully reassuring to the captain. Admiral Anson, in 1741, had been three hundred and fifty nautical miles out of his reckoning when he sighted the coast of South America at Cape Noir.

Mackenzie refers to the timepiece he took on his second voyage as an 'acrometer'. The word does not appear in dictionaries. The amusing suggestion that he was using a Greek prefix denoting negation to indicate that it did not in fact keep time is too subtle for anyone as straightforward as he. It may have been no more than a misspelling.

His timepiece being unreliable, Mackenzie needed some method of finding Greenwich time by looking into the sky above his own head. There were two methods in contemporary use and he employed them both, checking one against the other. With his sextant he could find the angle between the moon and some fixed star and, by consulting a table, reach approximate Greenwich time. This method is based on the fact that the moon, as it revolves about the earth, changes its apparent position relative to the fixed stars by about thirteen degrees in every twenty-four hours. From tables showing when the moon will be in a given position, it is possible to determine the time at Greenwich. Once that is known, a comparison with local time will determine one's longitude.

A second method is to observe a predictable astronomical event, of which the moment of occurrence, by Greenwich time, is already known and tabulated. The observation of the eclipses of the moons of the planet Jupiter provides a series of such known events. The only instruments required are sets of tables showing Greenwich time and a fairly large telescope. Mackenzie's telescope, which he had to carry over the mountains slung on his shoulder, was not as high powered as those which Cook and Vancouver had on shipboard, but seems to have been adequate.

Anyone reading Mackenzie's journal soon begins to wonder which of the two methods of fixing his position he gives preference to when they differ—astronomical observation or dead reckoning. The natural supposition is that he worked in the same way as David Thompson, who fixed

with his instruments the position of two points on his route
—ideally the beginning and end of a day's journey—and
then adjusted his record of the day's paddling or marching
accordingly. It comes as a surprise that Mackenzie was so
distrustful of his observations that when he made his map
he sometimes increased their error by adjusting them to his
dead reckoning. It has been noted that the watershed
between the Parsnip and the Fraser is shown on the map
fifteen miles east of where the observation for longitude re-
corded in his journal would locate it. The observation was
itself already twenty-five miles in error, in the same direction.
He was even capable of mis-correcting his latitude in the
same way.

All things considered, Mackenzie's performance in this
regard was very good indeed. For example, the course of the
Fraser shown on his map is generally accurate within ten
miles. Vancouver and Cook had far better instruments and
the advantage of a ship as a base, yet their longitudes for
Nootka differed by about fifteen miles and when Vancouver,
with immense care, was fixing the longitude of Monterey,
some of his sets of lunar observations were over twenty miles
out. He had the time and opportunity to make hundreds of
these and to correct one set against another whereas Mackenzie had to be continuously moving. In view of the rugged
country, the fatigues of travel through rapids and over portages, the alarms from Indians as he approached the coast
and, especially, the state of mind of his own men on 22 July
as, in imminent danger of attack, he took his last definitive
observations, we can only view his achievement with unquali-
fied admiration, heightened by the knowledge that, unlike
the ships' captains or the later Canadian surveyors, he had
never received a professional training.

As we follow Mackenzie's course, many of his observations

are omitted, for reasons of space and to avoid encumbering the narrative. The reader will find it easy to track his progress by reference to the maps provided.

In April, 1792, he left England and was back at Chipewyan in September. We do not know much about his doings during these months but he was at Grand Portage in July and probably told his partners in the Company of his westward intentions. It is certain that he offered a young clerk named McDonald the opportunity of joining the expedition to the Pacific, an offer which was not taken up.

At some time during the winter of 1791–2, he had arranged with Roderick to send a party up the Peace to cut timber for a post which would serve as a jumping-off point for the Pacific journey. This was to be still further upstream than the 'Old Establishment', a post established in 1788 by a man named Boyer.

Without doubt, Roderick had worked closely with his cousin in preparing for the new venture. By 10 October, Alexander was ready.

IV

Voyage to the Pacific

MACKENZIE's first voyage had been down the course of a
continuous waterway, to see where it led. His second expedition, designed to cross the watershed of the western
mountains and reach the Pacific Ocean, was an altogether
different matter. He must begin by going upstream, against
the current of the largest, most navigable river flowing out
of the Rockies. This was the Peace. Its waters, as they turned
north and, picking up the outflow of Lake Athabasca,
became the Slave River, had already carried him toward the
Arctic. Now he would go upstream to see where they came
from and would look for a navigable river running west.
Knowing that this might involve many delays and eager to
obtain all the information he could from Indians farther west
than Athabasca, he determined to winter on the Peace at
the extreme western limit of the country with which he was
familiar.

On 10 October 1792, the party set off and early on the
morning of 12 October entered the broad stream of the
Peace and pointed their prows westward. The weather was
cold and raw. On the 17th, they encountered falls twenty
feet high and made two portages. Several inches of snow fell
in the night. On the 18th, assisted by a north-east wind, they
made good progress, but it froze so hard during the night
that Mackenzie was afraid they would be stopped by ice.
They therefore set off at three o'clock the next morning and

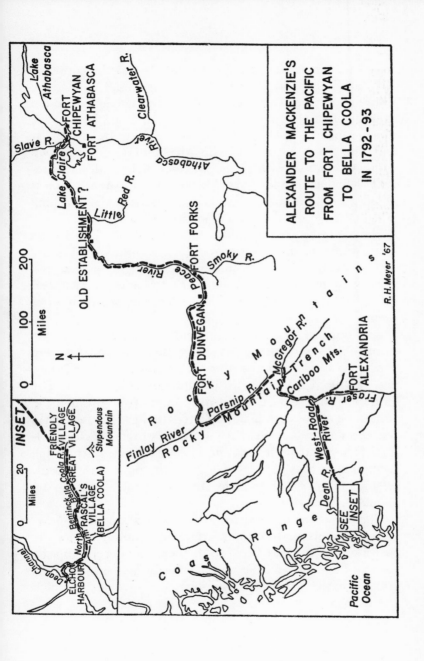

ALEXANDER MACKENZIE'S
ROUTE TO THE PACIFIC
FROM FORT CHIPEWYAN
TO BELLA COOLA
IN 1792-93

R.H. Meyer '67

Lake Athabasca
FORT CHIPEWYAN
FORT ATHABASCA
Clearwater R.
Slave R.
Athabasca River
Lake Claire
OLD ESTABLISHMENT ?
Little Red R.
FORT FORKS
Smoky R.
Peace River
FORT DUNVEGAN
Rocky Mountains
McGregor R.
Parsnip R.
Mountain Trench
Cariboo Mts.
Finlay River
Rocky
FORT ALEXANDRIA
Fraser R.
West-Road River
Dean R.
SEE INSET
Coast
Range
Pacific Ocean

0   100   200
Miles
N

INSET

FRIENDLY VILLAGE
Bella Coola R.
GREAT VILLAGE
North Bentinck
RASCAL'S VILLAGE
(BELLA COOLA)
Stupendous Mountain
ELCHO HARBOUR
Dean Channel

0   20
Miles

reached their destination about eight. It was the company fort called the Old Establishment. They were greeted by smoke and flame. The large house was burned down and the fire was proceeding fast to the smaller buildings. In the nick of time they leaped ashore and were able to put it out. It transpired that a party led by Mr Findlay, of their own company, had slept there the previous night and had carelessly left their fire burning. Mackenzie's apparently stoical acceptance of this minor disaster suggests his habit of keeping his mind fixed on one main objective.

Having overtaken Findlay, with his canoes, Mackenzie made a joint camp and prepared for a formal arrival at the new upstream post next morning. He had never seen any Indians from this area and, his plans depending a good deal on their friendliness, he was doubtless anxious to impress them.

At 6 a.m. on 20 October the joint party landed amid the firing of guns and other signs of rejoicing. The Indians were expecting a 'regale' and a nine-gallon cask of 'reduced rum' was produced, together with a quantity of tobacco. The gathering consisted of forty-two hunters. If we assume the rum to be of no more than half strength, at most, this works out at an average of less than a pint of rum for each individual. They had been awaiting it for six months, 'since the beginning of May; as it is a practice throughout the northwest neither to sell or give any rum to the natives during the summer'.

These Indians differed from the Chipewyans in appearance, manners and customs. Mackenzie notes, with some surprise, 'the contrast between the neat and decent appearance of the men, and the nastiness of the women.' He puts it down to the 'extreme submission and abasement' in which the women are kept.

On the morning of 23 October, fearing that he would be stopped by ice if he stayed any longer, he gave his last instructions to Findlay and made a speech to the Indians, then pushed off to the sound of 'several vollies of musketry' in his honour. After following the winding course¸ of the Peace for a week, he landed, on 1 November, at the place already chosen for his winter residence. Two canoes of stores, which he had sent on ahead, were already arrived and, although his men were exhausted and there was not a single hut to receive them, Mackenzie had a number of reasons to feel satisfied. Two men who had been up the previous spring to cut and square timber had done their work well. There were enough palisades eighteen feet long and seven inches in diameter to enclose a plot one hundred and twenty feet square. There were also timbers and planks stacked ready for the erection of a house. About seventy Indians, led by their chief, fired volley after volley to show their pleasure at his arrival. Mackenzie distributed small amounts of tobacco and rum, lighted the pipe which was a sign of peaceful discussion, and announced that while he knew they had been troublesome to his predecessor, he would treat them with kindness and justice. In return they made 'the fairest promises; and having expressed the pride they felt on beholding me in their country, took their leave'. By 7 November, he had finished dealing with the Indians; he had taken great care to equip them for their winter hunting, as his party would depend on them for fresh meat. He now turned his attention to getting the palisades erected and dwellings and storehouses built. On 27 November the frost was so severe that the axes of the workmen became almost as brittle as glass. The next day at 8 a.m. his Fahrenheit thermometer registered 16° below zero. A few days later it was accidentally broken, so there is no further record. Mackenzie was now settling down for the winter. On 23 December he moved from his tent into the first of the new houses to be erected and set all hands to work on five more, of about seventeen by twelve feet.

The Indians in this wild region were apparently without a knowledge of healing herbs and Mackenzie involuntarily found himself the authority on medical matters. A woman with a swelled breast 'which had been lacerated with flint stones for the cure of it' he cured by means of cleanliness, poultices and a healing salve. One of his own men contracted blood poisoning and was in extreme pain. As a last resort Mackenzie ventured to let some blood and the man soon made a complete recovery.

Slowly the winter wore away. At break of day on 1 January the New Year was greeted by a discharge of fire-arms from the men. Spirits were dealt out and cakes made of flour—a special treat.

Several times during the winter the warm south-west wind blew, snow melted and water flooded the ice. This wind, the famed 'Chinook', came from the direction of the Pacific and Mackenzie concluded that the distance from salt water, in a straight line, was so short that, although the wind passed over mountains covered with snow there was not time for it to cool. It was a shrewd observation and shows how alert he was to anything that related to the success of his journey. He could not be expected to know that these south-west winds were relatively warm and dry because they had shed their load of moisture on the west side of successive ranges and by their very descent from the high ridges had become compressed and warmed.

Mackenzie was naturally more at leisure to record his thoughts and observations at this time than he would be when actually travelling and he has a good deal to say about the Indians, his own voyageurs and the surrounding country. It is evident that his men, often referred to as 'my people', are in a special relation to him, more like the relation of clansmen to chief than of servants to master. 'The men who are with me,' he tells us, 'left this place in the beginning of last May, and went to the Rainy Lake in canoes, laden with packs of fur, which, from the immense length of the voyage, and other concurring circumstances, is a most severe trial of patience and perseverance: there they do not remain a sufficient time for ordinary repose, when they take a load of goods in exchange, and proceed on their return, in a great measure, day and night. They had been arrived near two months, and, all that time, had been continually engaged in very toilsome labour, with nothing more than a common shed to protect them from the frost and snow. Such is the life which these people lead; and is continued with unremitting exertion, till their strength is lost in premature old age.'

With all its hardship, the lot of the voyageur was a good deal better than that of the Indian. The bands Mackenzie was dealing with seem to have been pushed out this far to the north and west by more warlike Cree and Beaver. Their social organization was feeble and their state must have been one of permanent insecurity. Yet they were not without virtues of courage, endurance, generosity and gratitude. When all is said, they remain mysterious.

At considerable length, Mackenzie records how, upon his arrival, a young Indian was brought to him whose gun had burst some time before and whose thumb hung by a small strip of flesh. The wound was in an appalling condition, his friends having done nothing in the way of treatment beyond singing about him and blowing on his hand. Mackenzie, in considerable alarm, poulticed it with the bark of spruce roots, succeeded finally in amputating the thumb, concocted a salve of balsam, wax and tallow and after about two months of treatment found that his patient had been able to join a hunting party and now presented him with the tongue of an elk, as a token of gratitude.

The hardships and debasement of the Indian women in this region seem to have impressed Mackenzie very unfavourably. 'It is not uncommon, while the men carrying nothing but a gun, that their wives and daughters follow with such weighty burdens, that if they lay them down they cannot replace them, and that is a kindness which the men will not deign to perform; so that during their journeys they are frequently obliged to lean against a tree for a small portion of temporary relief.' 'It is by no means uncommon in the hasty removal of their camps from one position to another, for a woman to be taken in labour, to deliver herself in her way, without any assistance or notice from her associates in the journey, and to overtake them before they complete the arrangements of their evening station, with her new-born babe on her back.' With such general insensitiveness there could also exist a superstitious sense of guilt for acts of barbarism. An Indian who five years earlier had largely lost the use of his legs came to Mackenzie for a remedy. 'This affliction he attributed to his cruelty about that time, when having found a wolf with two whelps in an old beaver lodge, he set fire to it and consumed them.'

In the early part of April Mackenzie was busy trading furs, repairing old canoes with bark and building four new ones. He fulfilled his duty to the company by sending six canoes loaded with furs, on 8 May, back to Fort Chipewyan. Six voyageurs remained; they had agreed to go with him on his projected voyage of discovery.

During the winter, he made several observations of Jupiter

to fix his longitude and found it to be 117° 35' 15" West. His
'acrometer' was one hour and forty-six minutes slow and he
established that it lost an average of twenty seconds in
twenty-four hours. 'Having settled this point, the canoe was
put into the water: her dimensions were twenty-five feet long
within, exclusive of curves of stem and stern, twenty-six
inches hold, and four feet nine inches beam.' His chronometer and his canoe were two precision instruments, the one
as carefully checked and calculated as the other. The canoe
was so light that on a good portage two men could carry her
three or four miles without resting. Yet she held three thousand pounds of provisions, goods for presents, arms, ammunition and baggage, together with ten people. Two of them,
Joseph Landry and Charles Ducette, had been to the Arctic
with him. The others were Francois Beaulieux, Baptiste
Bisson, Francois Courtois, Jacques Beauchamp, Alexander
Mackay and two Indians as hunters and interpreters. Mackay
appears a kind of second-in-command. The small group left
in charge of the fort 'shed tears on the reflection of those
dangers which we might encounter in our expedition, while
my own people offered up their prayers that we might return
in safety from it'.

Fort Fork, which they were leaving, was situated a few
miles west of the spot where the Smoky River joins the Peace.
Between them and the Pacific surf lay five hundred miles of
mountains, covered with bush that would make every mile
on foot a struggle to advance. At the moment they were
paddling against a strong but unimpeded current. Mackenzie
knew, however, that he was ascending a watershed and
would have to find his way across the divide and search for
a navigable stream running generally west. An Indian who
seemed to have positive knowledge of a large river flowing
south and west had disappeared just before the expedition

started. He had said that the two rivers came within two days' journey of each other.

The expedition set off on the evening of Thursday, 9 May, and, as was customary, moved only a few miles before making their first camp. An early start was made the next morning but the canoe, which appears to have been overloaded, began to leak. At noon they had to land, unload and gum the seams. Mackenzie took an altitude and found they were at 55° 58′ 48″ North latitude. As they continued their course, he unluckily dropped his pocket compass into the water, an annoying but not crippling loss. Early in the evening they landed to camp for the night and the young men succeeded in killing an elk and wounding a buffalo. It is improbable that anyone was troubled by this latter fact except in so far as it cost them some meat.

On the 11th, 12th and 13th they were in uneasy contact with a hunting party of Beaver Indians. Mackenzie was afraid they would discourage his own Indians from continuing with him. He anxiously inquired after an old man of the tribe whom he had talked to at the fort but no one knew where he was. The old man had described to him a river which forked into two branches and had directed him to take the southern branch, which would bring him close to the river flowing west, to within 'about a day's march for a young man'. These two tremendous tributaries, coming one from the north, the other from the south, and joining in the mountain trench to form the main stream of the Peace, Mackenzie was soon to discover. The old man's description, unlike so much that he had heard, was accurate. On Monday, 13 May, they parted from the band.

Mackenzie's fear that his Indians might desert had not been groundless. The eldest of them told him that the previous night his uncle had lamented his running into the dangers ahead but that he had answered, the Chief required his services and he must follow. How well Mackenzie's built-in attitudes and expectations of receiving as well as giving loyalty served him was once more demonstrated.

His observations of scenery, of flora and fauna, were sometimes purely appreciative of their natural beauty but generally very shrewdly aware of their value to the fur trader. On Wednesday, 15 May, he observes, 'In an island which we passed, there was a large quantity of white birch, whose bark might be employed in the construction of canoes.' The next day they came to Sinew River, so named by the Rocky Mountain Indians, and he notes, 'This spot would be an excellent situation for a fort or factory, as there is plenty of wood, and every reason to believe that the country abounds in beaver.' That day they saw 'two grisly and hideous bears'. Grizzly bears were new to Mackenzie as they were only to be found in the mountains. They were the terror of travellers because they were much more courageous than most bears and would attack without hesitation. Large, fierce, and from their grizzled appearance terrifying, they received the scientific name of *Ursus horribilis.*

Next day, Friday, 17 May, the Rocky Mountains heaved into view, south-west by south, their summits a welcome and encouraging sight, appearing sooner than anyone expected. They landed for the night at seven, their usual hour, and Mackay took a shot at a buffalo, when his gun burst, but fortunately near the muzzle and no one was hurt. The next three days were consumed in a protracted struggle against a series of rapids, cascades and falls. The banks were often perpendicular or overhanging; stones were continually rolling down to imperil those dragging the canoe; they had to portage through a forest of spruce, birch and the largest poplars Mackenzie had ever seen. On the Monday they set off at a quarter past four and found themselves facing rapids bordered by a cliff so steep that Mackenzie had to cut steps for twenty feet, then leap down to a small rock in the river and receive those who followed one by one on his shoulders. Four of them having passed in this way, they attempted to pull up the canoe. It broke under the strain. Mending it required a fire to melt the mixture of gum and tallow with which the seams had to be payed. By good luck a dead tree had fallen from the cliff and served their purpose. At the next point they were able to embark and to reach a small sandy bay sheltered by a round high island of stone. Certain that worse still was to come, they sent out two men to look for birch bark with which extensive repairs could be made. The men soon returned but Mackay and the Indians with him were cut off from the canoe by broken ground and could not man a tow line. The crew of the canoe now worked it forward with the aid of poles till they came beneath a precipice where the depth of the water made poling impossible. As a last resort, a tow line was carried to the top of the cliff and the men handling it scrambled precariously round the outside of trees that grew on the edge of the precipice. 'We however, surmounted this difficulty, as we had done many others.'

They now had to make a traverse so difficult that some of the voyageurs stripped themselves to their shirts, fearing they would capsize. But this too was accomplished. After negotiating a cascade by partly unloading, Mackenzie stopped at noon to take an altitude. In the midst of the operation, the canoe, negligently tied, was almost lost as it swung into the current. And a cloud covered the sun. Nevertheless, he got a reading of 56° North latitude which was later proved 'tolerably correct'.

Within the next two miles they were obliged to unload four

times, and with the utmost difficulty prevented the canoe from being dashed to pieces. Then the river became one continuous rapid, 'a wave striking on the bow of the canoe broke the line, and filled us with inexpressible dismay, as it appeared impossible that the vessel could escape from being dashed to pieces, and those who were in her from perishing', yet miraculously a great swell lifted her over the rocks and she came to shore relatively undamaged. The men, however, were shaken by this series of narrow escapes and the river was one white sheet of broken water as far as could be seen. Mackenzie camped for the night. The men were muttering that there was nothing for it but to return, but he at once set off with one Indian, to reconnoitre, ordering the rest to get to the top of the bank, an ascent so steep they were obliged to fell trees on the declivity.

On Tuesday, 21 May, Mackay, with three voyageurs and two Indians, went on ahead to look for the end of the rapids. They returned in the evening saying that rough and thickly wooded country lay before. It would be better, for the next nine miles, to go by land and not by water. But a kettle of wild rice, sweetened with sugar, and their usual regale of rum soon produced a more cheerful atmosphere. At break of day they began with axes to cut a road through the bush up the side of the mountain and by evening they had not only warped the canoe up to the top with a rope and brought up all the baggage but had also cleared a path for another mile ahead.

At ten the weather cleared and Mackenzie could satisfy himself as to their position. 'I observed an emersion of Jupiter's second sattelite; time by the acrometer 8·32·20 by which I found the longitude to be 120·29·30. West from Greenwich.'

During the next two days, the party covered a distance of

about seven miles, laboriously clearing a road through the forest. At first they merely enlarged a 'well-beaten elk path'; then a burned over area in which briars were mixed with a criss-cross of fallen trunks confronted them. Here, too, they encountered the bois-picant, now known as devil's club, which they had not met before. 'It rises to about nine feet in height, grows in joints without branches, and is tufted at the extremity. The stem is of an equal size from the bottom to the top, and does not exceed an inch in diameter; it is covered with small prickles, which caught our trowsers, and working through them, sometimes found their way to the flesh.'

They were now past the canyon and, in spite of their efforts, had not yet come to the Rocky Mountains proper. How difficult it was to travel in this groping fashion, without maps or reliable information, comes out in Mackenzie's remark, 'But after all, the Indian carrying way, whatever may be its length, and I think it cannot exceed ten miles, will always be found more safe and expeditious than the passage which our toil and perseverance formed and surmounted.' He could not have anticipated that his passage would get worse as he ascended the canyon. The information he got from Indians was a mixture of true and false. At every point he had to rely on his own judgment or instinct.

During the next few days they passed through the Rocky Mountains. Mackenzie's careful notations of distance and direction are missing. 'I lost the book that contained them. I was in the habit of sometimes indulging myself with a short doze in the canoe, and I imagine that the branches of the trees brushed my book from me, when I was in such a situation.'

On 29 May it rained with such continuous violence that they could not proceed. Mackenzie amused himself by writing an account of their hardships and successes, wrapping it in bark and putting it through the bung-hole of a rum keg which they had just emptied. 'Which being carefully secured, I consigned this epistolary cargo to the mercy of the current.' It has been calculated that, if the keg were the usual five-gallon size, the men had been consuming one-fifth of a pint per day. Cold and wet as they often were, it must have been a welcome tot.

They were in harsh and difficult terrain. Mountain torrents, white and milky with the rock dust of the glaciers and swollen with melting snow, poured into the main stream. On 31 May, 'At nine the men were so cold that we landed, in order to kindle a fire, which was considered as a very uncommon circumstance at this season; a small quantity of rum, however, served as an adequate substitute; and the current being so smooth as to admit the use of paddles, I encouraged them to proceed without any further delay.' They pushed on and reached 'a beautiful sheet of water, that was heightened by the calmness of the weather, and a splendid sun'. Beyond this lay more rapids and the daunting evidence that their hope of a straight run to the sea once the Rockies were past, was not to be realized. 'Here the view convinced us that our late hopes were without foundation, as there appeared a ridge or chain of mountains, running South and North as far as the eye could reach.' Nothing in Mackenzie's experience, though he had been born in Scotland and had traversed so much of North America, would have prepared him for the fact that he was facing a wild tossing sea of high mountains and plateaux ending only when the last sunken ranges were covered by the waters of the Pacific.

A few miles farther on, he had to make a crucial decision as to their direction. The Peace forked at this point into a stream coming in from west-north-west and one from south-south-east. These rivers are now called the Finlay and the Parsnip. 'If I had been governed by my own judgment, I should have taken the former, as it appeared to me to be the most likely to bring us nearest to the part where I wished to fall on the Pacific Ocean; but the old man, whom I have already mentioned as having been frequently on war expeditions in this country, had warned me not, on any account, to follow it, as it was soon lost in various branches among the mountains, and that there was no great river that ran in any direction near it; but by following the latter, he said, we should arrive at a carrying-place to another large river, that did not exceed a day's march, where the inhabitants build houses, and live upon islands. There was so much apparent truth in the old man's narrative, that I determined to be governed by it; for I did not entertain the least doubt, if I could get into the other river, that I should reach the ocean.' Once again we can but admire Mackenzie's perspicacity. Had he gone up the Finlay, he would have been in such rough country and so far from navigable waters leading west it is very doubtful that he could ever have reached his objective. The Parsnip, however, was the harder river to ascend; against a powerful current it took most of the afternoon to get two or three miles upstream. The crew and the Indians were much discouraged and their leader had to perform the classic role of inspiring hope and courage into his followers: 'the inexpressible toil these people had endured, as well as the dangers they had encountered, required some degree of consideration; I therefore employed those arguments which were the best calculated to calm their immediate discontents, as well as to encourage their future hopes, though, at the same time, I delivered my sentiments in such a manner as to convince them that I was determined to proceed.' It is at a point like this that we must use all our powers of imagination and reconstruction if we are to see this group of chilled and exhausted voyageurs and Indians, whose native languages are not Mackenzie's, pitching camp on the bank of a turbulent stream which he alone thinks is worth ascending and to sense their total discouragement. His unrivalled powers of persuasion were once more successful, for the next morning, 1 June, they embarked at sunrise.

The next night brought fresh discomforts. The Indians, who had been on foot in the bush in order to lighten the canoe, were certain they heard more musket shots than could be accounted for and that a war party of Knisteneaux (Crees) must be in the vicinity. 'Our fusees were, therefore, primed and loaded, and, having extinguished our fire, each of us took his station at the foot of a tree, where we passed an uneasy and restless night.' They were in a tract full of beaver which could be seen in great numbers and had felled many acres of large poplars to build their dams and lodges.

The account we have of the next two days, 4 and 5 June, reveals Mackenzie and some of the reasons why he succeeded. He strove, not merely to establish at frequent intervals his latitude and longitude, but also to keep a record of his course by compass. Not even Cook and Vancouver, in the context of their kind of navigation, could have been more thorough. In the midst of dangers, violent exertions and distractions, he was keeping laborious note of his slow progress. For 4 June we read: 'Our course was this day, South-South-East one mile, South-South-West half a mile, South-East three quarters of a mile, North-East by East three quarters of a mile, South-East half a mile, South-East by South one mile, South-South-East one mile three quarters, South-East by South half a mile, East by South a quarter of a mile, South-East three quarters of a mile, North-East by East half a mile,

East by North a quarter of a mile, South-East half a mile, South-East by South a quarter of a mile, South-East by East half a mile, North-East by East half a mile, North-North-East three quarters of a mile, and South by East one mile and an half.' In spite of one lost notebook, he was in a position to recall each turn, as the thread of his progress was stretching into this labyrinth of mountains. The Indians around him were often scarcely aware of what lay on the far side of the next visible range. At the same time, their own stone-age equipment was adequate to ensure their survival. The gulf between two such disparate cultures could not be bridged. But the fur traders straddled it to the extent of learning how to make canoes and live on the country and they persuaded the Indian that it was to his profit to sell his furs.

The next day, 5 June, demonstrated how completely their progress was governed by Mackenzie's single will. Having gummed the seams of the canoe, which their hasty, belated encampment on a precarious gravel bank had prevented, they crossed over to the north shore of the river. Here Mackenzie and Mackay, together with the Indian hunters, disembarked. The voyageurs were to continue upstream while the others climbed a mountain to get a view of the terrain, the Indians, of course, being also on the lookout for game. 'I directed my people to proceed with all possible diligence, and that, if they met with any accident, or found my return necessary, they should fire two guns. They also understood, that when they should hear the same signal from me they were to answer, and wait for me, if I were behind them.' Having climbed the hill, Mackenzie found the forest so thick that, to get any sense of the surrounding country, he was obliged, himself, to climb a very lofty tree, from which vantage point he could see a snow-covered range to the north-west and another ridge, without snow, running from north to south. The trench, between these latter heights and the Rockies he had just come through, was clearly the course of the river they were following. Returning to the bank, they fired twice as agreed. No answer. Crossing a point of land, they obtained a long view of the river. There was nothing in sight. They fired again, as agreed, and Mackay and one Indian were left, to build a signal fire and drift broken branches downstream as signs. Mackenzie and the other Indian pushed upstream through intense heat and over loose sand. They returned to find Mackay had made a similar trip downstream and without result. The Indians were now planning how to return home by building a raft. 'As for myself, it will be easily believed, that my mind was in a state of extreme agitation; and the imprudence of my conduct in leaving the people in such a situation of danger and toilsome exertion, added a very painful mortification to the severe apprehensions I already suffered: it was an act of indiscretion which might have put an end to the voyage that I had so much at heart, and compelled me at length to submit to the scheme which my hunters had already formed for our return.' After prolonged further search, Mackenzie and his Indian were preparing to spend the night in the open when shots announced that Mackay had made contact with the canoe. Mackenzie who had drunk a great deal of cold water, with no food, would willingly have stayed the night where he was, but his Indian complained so bitterly that they set off and by nightfall, barefooted and soaked with rain, hungry and exhausted, they reached the canoe. 'But these inconveniences affected me very little, when I saw myself once more sur-rounded with my people. They informed me, that the canoe had been broken, and that they had this day experienced much greater toil and hardships than on any former occasion.

I thought it prudent to affect a belief of every representation that they made, and even to comfort each of them with a consolatory dram: for, however difficult the passage might have been, it was too short to have occupied the whole day, if they had not relaxed in their exertions. The rain was accompanied with thunder and lightning.'

Even through the screen of this formal prose, one can clearly visualize the scene. The Indians, anxious to return as soon as possible. The voyageurs, incomparable in their loyalty and endurance, yet without their leader's driving determination. Mackay, the somewhat shadowy *fidus Achates*, about whom we would dearly like to know more. Mackenzie himself, fully in control, providing rum and sympathy, concealing his vexation, glad that tomorrow is another day and that his expedition, materially and in morale, was still intact. It rained, against a backdrop of thunder and lightning. They continued their journey at half past four the next morning.

During the next few days, the Indians, who disliked the labour of navigating the canoe, were as much as possible on shore, in search of game, but without much success. Supper on 8 June consisted of the boiled tops of wild parsnips mixed with pemmican. Mackenzie had been anxiously hoping for some contact with local Indians who might know where the portages ahead were located and the next day they encountered a band of Sekani, who had heard of white men but never before seen any. It took two or three hours for Mackenzie, through his interpreter, to persuade them to let him land peaceably and talk to them all. They amounted to only three men, three women and seven or eight boys and girls and seemed wretchedly ill equipped. Mackenzie had, in fact, stumbled on some members of a most unfortunate tribe, who lived in a district poor in game between two stronger tribes, Beavers who had driven them across the Rockies and, on the west, Carriers, from whom they got some iron but no guns. Mackenzie exerted himself to gain their confidence, even giving them some of his cherished pemmican, which was superior to their dried fish, while the children got some sugar. He was determined to find out all they might know of the hoped for river flowing westward into the Pacific. He was in a difficult crux, for lack of any sense of what lay just before him. Should he leave the canoe and travel westward overland? This he concluded to be impossible, as the party could not carry the weight of provisions, goods for presents and ammunition required. Should he continue and risk finding himself with his supplies depleted, somewhere up at the headwaters of the Parsnip with no way out of the mountains? Should he return to the forks and try the Finlay? He could not bring himself to think of giving up: 'to return unsuccessful, after all our labour, sufferings and dangers, was an idea too painful to indulge'. He was doubtful, too, whether his interpreter, who was very tired of the voyage, was accurately translating all that the Sekani were telling him. So far they had seemed to deny the existence of any river that would serve his purpose. It was a most critical juncture, at which the smallest failure of nerve, of will or of judgment might have brought total collapse of the expedition. He quietly persisted in trying to gain the confidence of the natives and one of them brought him five beaver skins, as a present; others produced dried fish.

Next morning he renewed the conversation but without learning anything new from the Sekani. 'About nine, however, one of them, still remaining at my fire, in conversation with the interpreters, I understood enough of his language to know that he mentioned something about a great river, at the same time pointing significantly up that which was before us.' This great river, he learned, flowed to the south; one of its tributaries could be reached from the headwaters of the river he was now navigating; the great river did not empty itself into the sea. With a piece of charcoal on a strip of bark, the Indian sketched out what he had described, making Mackenzie's heart leap with impatient hope. He could not know that this river had an immense canyon full of rapids, which no Indian would have much reason to risk his neck in, searching for salt water, but he did correctly infer that no great river in these longitudes could end anywhere but in the Pacific.

With renewed hope, Mackenzie quickly induced one of the Sekani to act as a guide to the next band they might meet and within an hour the party was on its way, promising to return within two moons. The five beaver skins were returned to their donor with the promise that they would be picked up and paid for on the way back.

The next morning, 11 June, was clear and cold. The guide, when urged not to desert them by night, replied through the interpreter, 'How is it possible for me to leave the lodge of the Great Spirit? When he tells me that he has no further occasion for me, I will then return to my children.' Through the triple screen of interpreter, Mackenzie himself and William Combe, we can hear what sounds like a nice tribute to Mackenzie's powers of persuasion. 'As we proceeded, however, he soon lost, and with good reason, his exalted notions of me.' It is clear that Mackenzie had no wish to pose as an exalted being; indeed, it would be difficult to do so in a battered and leaking canoe which they now had to spend over an hour patching up with gum. They left the Parsnip and entered a creek which took them to a small lake.

Up between three and four the next morning, they found half a dozen fish in the net that had been set overnight. Food was a constant preoccupation. They had now reached the Continental Divide and were the first Europeans to cross it north of the Spanish territories of the remote south-west. They were in a pass, a quarter of a mile wide, between two rocky precipices. Eight hundred and seventeen paces of portage brought them to another small lake, whose waters flowed west toward the Pacific. It was an Indian carrying-place; old canoes lay there and on the trees hung baskets containing articles left for later use. They helped themselves to a net, some hooks, the horn of a mountain goat and a wooden trap, leaving in exchange a knife, some fire-steels, beads, awls, etc. It will be noted how compact and portable everything is which the party carries. Unlike African travellers, they are their own porters.

They were now hindered by driftwood and fallen trees. Indeed the advantage they had acquired, of going with the stream instead of against it, was cancelled by the rugged and thickly forested terrain. Two men sent forward to reconnoitre 'brought back a fearful detail of rapid currents, fallen trees, and large stones'. Their guide was now very anxious to go home. The rapids they had gone down had greatly alarmed him.

The next day, 13 June, was a day of calamity. The current ran with great rapidity. To lighten the canoe, Mackenzie decided that he and some others should walk. 'But those in the boat with great earnestness requested me to embark, declaring, at the same time, that, if they perished, I should perish with them. I did not then imagine in how short a period their apprehension would be justified.' They had scarcely started when the canoe struck, was driven sideways, and broke itself on a sandbar. They all jumped out but were immediately swept into deeper water and had to scramble back for their lives, leaving one man behind. The torrent then drove them into a rock, shattering the stern below the gunwales, so that the steersman could no longer keep his place. Thrown to the opposite side of the channel, the canoe similarly smashed its bow. In the hope of checking their course, the foreman seized the branches of a small tree but was himself jerked violently ashore while the canoe swept on into a cascade which tore great holes in the bark and dislocated the thwarts so that the wreck floated flat on the water. Panic stricken, the steersman called on his companions to save themselves but Mackenzie's peremptory commands prevailed and they all held fast to the wreck, which alone saved them from being individually dashed against the rocks. 'In this condition we were forced several hundred yards, and every yard on the verge of destruction; but, at length, we most fortunately arrived in shallow water and a small eddy, where we were enabled to make a stand, from the weight of the canoe resting on the stones, rather than from any exertions of our exhausted strength. For though our efforts were short, they were pushed to the utmost, as life or death depended on them.' The foreman, who had escaped unhurt, now appeared, to give his assistance. The Indians made no effort to help but sat down and wept. Mackenzie held the canoe on the outside till everything was got on shore. He was in great pain from the icy water and finally came ashore so benumbed he could hardly stand and badly bruised. Among their losses was their total spare supply of bullets. But, as the absent man appeared, their sole thought was of the miraculous preservation of the whole party.

Mackenzie's task was now the one familiar to all readers of Homer's *Odyssey*. He listened in silence to suggestions inspired by a panic desire to abandon the voyage. Not until the warmth and comfort of a fire, a hearty meal and an allowance of rum had taken effect did he begin to rebuild morale.

'I then addressed them, by recommending them all to be thankful for their late very narrow escape. I also stated, that the navigation was not impracticable in itself, but from our ignorance of its course; and that our late experience would enable us to pursue our voyage with greater security. I brought to their recollection, that I did not deceive them, and that they were made acquainted with the difficulties and dangers they must expect to encounter, before they engaged to accompany me. I also urged the honour of conquering disasters, and the disgrace that would attend them on their return home, without having attained the object of the expedition. Nor did I fail to mention the courage and resolution which was the peculiar boast of the North men; and that I depended on them, at that moment, for the maintenance of their character. I quieted their apprehension as to the loss of the bullets, by bringing to their recollection that we still had shot from which they might be manufactured. I at the same time acknowledged the difficulty of restoring the wreck of the canoe, but confided in our skill and exertion to put it in such a state as would carry us on to where we might procure bark, and build a new one. In short, my harangue produced the desired effect, and a very general assent appeared to go wherever I should lead the way.' This is in the great classical tradition; neither Odysseus nor Caesar, exhorting his legionaries, could have done a better job. Whatever words Mackenzie actually said to his voyageurs, or his interpreter to the Indians, the result of inspiriting the discouraged and gaining over the disaffected, was visibly accomplished. By nine the next morning a party had set out to bring back birch bark and to look for their junction with the expected great river.

Here Mackenzie made one of his many observations to establish their position. His latitude appeared to be 54° 23′

but he could not get a sufficient horizon, among the mountains, to try for the satellites of Jupiter. He did determine that his chronometer was running slow.

That evening one of the Indians brought in a small roll of poor bark. The next morning the other two members of the exploring party came in hungry, cold and exhausted, their clothes torn to tatters and their skin lacerated from their struggle through the woods. They believed they had found the great river, or a branch of it. They could see no way of reaching it, however, because of obstructions in the stream the party was now on, except by carrying the canoe the whole way across this appalling terrain, where a path would have to be cut with great labour through the bush. They were fortunate, however, in having anyone to listen to their story, for during their absence eighty pounds of gunpowder had been spread out 'to receive the air; and, in this situation, one of the men carelessly and composedly walked across it with a lighted pipe in his mouth, but without any ill consequence resulting from such an act of criminal negligence. I need not add that one spark might have put a period to all my anxiety and ambition.'

The poor shattered canoe was now pieced together with the aid of some indifferent bark, several pieces of oil-cloth and plenty of gum, and next morning, 15 June, it proceeded downstream, guided by four men and lightened of its load by about half a ton. The men were a little more cheerful now, though one of them, Jacques Beauchamp, refused absolutely to embark. It was the first example of absolute disobedience during the voyage and Mackenzie met it with tact and judgment. Beauchamp was a good voyageur, active and hardworking, but his companions regarded him as a rather simple soul. Mackenzie therefore took the line that he was so ridiculous as not to be worth taking any further

Rafted ice piled fifteen feet high in June on bank of Mackenzie River
J. R. Mackay

Peace River Canyon
British Columbia Government photograph

Peace River, fifty miles west of the British
Columbia boundary
British Columbia Government photograph

on the voyage. How skilful, in general, were Mackenzie's methods of restoring morale, was demonstrated the same evening. 'At the close of the day we assembled round a blazing fire, and the whole party, being enlivened with the usual beverage which I supplied on these occasions, forgot their fatigues and apprehensions; nor did they fail to anticipate the pleasure they should enjoy in getting clear of their present difficulties, and gliding onwards with a strong and steady stream, which our guide had described as the characteristic of the large river we soon expected to enter.' Once again we hear the echo of captains and commanders throughout history who have known the secret of inspiring the doubtful and inspiriting the weary among their followers.

Next day the toilsome journey was continued. Some cleared a narrow path, others carried the packages, the rest guided the canoe through rapids. Soon a hole was torn in the bottom, then falls appeared over which no canoe could pass. Through deep mud filled with roots and criss-crossed with fallen trees the canoe was slowly carried forward; it was now so heavy with its patchings that two men could not carry it more than a hundred yards without being relieved. Their progress for the day was about two miles. Mackay and one of the Indians returned from a reconnaissance ahead with a dismal tale of morasses, almost impenetrable bush and the river, in its lower course, choked with driftwood. They had almost lost the dog, which fell in and was swept under the logs. At three o'clock the next morning, Mackay being on watch, Mackenzie woke to find that their interpreter was gone. He had had his fill of hardships and dangers.

During the following day, 17 June, they alternately paddled and portaged, sometimes wading in mud thigh deep and by eight o'clock, to their vast relief, reached the bank of the great river they were in search of. It was tributary to the still larger stream and the next night found them camped some thirty miles below the junction—of the McGregor and the Fraser as they are now called.

Mackenzie was eager to get in contact with local Indians. For several days they had seen the smoke of fires. On 19 June a campfire was seen ahead, right on the shore, but its owners fled when the canoe approached and, as they retreated, shot five arrows at Mackenzie's two Indians, who followed in hopes of communicating with them. The languages were 'mutually unintelligible'.

This was a country very different from anything Mackenzie had experienced east of the Rockies or on the divide. The Indians were Carriers and lived largely on salmon; huge firs and cedars gave evidence of a milder climate and more abundant rainfall; they killed two red deer of a species— mule deer—not before encountered. On 20 June they landed at a deserted house of a kind Mackenzie had not seen since he left Michilimackinac, at the junction of Lake Huron and Lake Michigan. It was about thirty feet by twenty, with three doors and three fireplaces. He had come into a country where abundant timber, a reliable food supply and a relatively temperate climate gave the native inhabitants a high standard of living. A cylindrical wooden fish trap fifteen feet long and four and a half feet in diameter was stored in this long house, which was clearly a seasonal dwelling. Other houses were seen as they continued downstream.

Contact with the local Indians, a new canoe to replace the shattered and patched frame they had under them, and some calculation of food needed for their return journey: now that they were over the divide and in navigable waters, these needs were in the forefront of Mackenzie's mind.

The canoe was almost too heavy to carry and with some reluctance he gave way to the wishes of the men and allowed them to run it unloaded down the next rapids, with the result that it swamped and three hours was lost before they were in a condition to proceed. During the day, four men had been sent out to look for bark and had brought back enough to sheathe a new frame.

Next day, 21 June, ninety pounds of pemmican was cached in a deep hole. The usual practice was followed of building a fire over the spot, to obliterate the signs of digging and to discourage animal predators. They were now moving south and the latitude was observed as 52° 47′ 51″. They steered past cliffs of blue and yellow clay, looking like ruins of old castles, and Mackenzie's hope of contact with natives was raised as he saw a small new canoe drawn up to the edge of the woods and, soon after, another with a man in it coming out of a little tributary.

The man gave a whoop of alarm and his friends immediately appeared, armed with bows and arrows and spears. They threatened the party, shouting that they would be instantly killed if they tried to land. The Indians with Mackenzie, who could understand this language, tried to pacify them, but without success. A volley of arrows, some of which fell short while others whistled overhead, left no doubt as to their hostility. Why these natives, high on the Pacific slope, should be so much more hostile than those Mackenzie had encountered on the Peace or in Athabasca is not entirely clear. It seems likely that many of the wandering bands further north and east were themselves victims of aggression and conscious of being in a sense fugitive. They would be more likely to flee than to attack and generally more tentative and open to persuasion in any negotiation. It is possible, too, that even this far from the Pacific the evil odour of the maritime fur trade was known. The crews of vessels collecting sea otter and seal pelts were often little better than pirates; they employed barter, trickery and violence indiscriminately.

Mackenzie's response to the immediate situation was superb. Seeing a canoe with two men depart downstream, probably to raise the alarm and get help, he determined to forestall this and, without showing, or allowing his men to show, any sign of fear, he coolly landed and walked alone along the beach. As usual, he gauged the exact line between foolhardiness and timidity. His plan worked to perfection. Seeing that he was alone and without a musket, and hearing the interpreter call out that no harm was intended to them, two of the natives came over in a canoe to within a hundred yards of Mackenzie. He displayed some looking glasses and other trinkets and made signs for them to land. With much hesitation and in evident fear, they finally came and sat by him. One of his own Indians, who had been instructed to shadow him, in case he should be attacked, now came out from the trees and joined them. He was able to communicate without difficulty, although he was by tribe a Beaver. Finally, after the two bolder locals had crossed back and reported, Mackenzie's whole party was invited into the encampment. Trinkets were distributed and some sugar for the children. Mackenzie, through the interpreters, then tried to find what lay ahead. The reports were by no means reassuring.

He was told that the river—which for convenience we shall continue to call the Fraser—was very long and flowed to the south. Rumour said that at its mouth white people were building houses. In three places the strong current was impassable, because of falls and rapids, while the perpendicular cliffs, higher and more rugged than anything the party had yet seen, made portaging impossible. The inhabitants were numerous and those just downstream were a malignant race that lived underground. If the party were to attempt the journey to the sea, they would be killed. The inhabitants possessed arms, which they secured from others to the west, who in turn got them from white men, who came in huge canoes.

Aware that he was getting a mixture of true and false information and considerably disturbed by some of it, Mackenzie was nevertheless eager to press on immediately and was in the act of persuading two of the band to come with him when, from downstream, a canoe carrying three more appeared, one of them a middle-aged Indian with an air of authority. He persuaded Mackenzie to stay until the next day.

The band was composed of seven families, containing eighteen men. They had come to this spot to spend the summer and were building fish traps of the kind Mackenzie had already seen. In appearance, language and manners they were similar to the Indians already encountered in the Rockies. They were clothed in leather and had some blankets of beaver and of rabbit skin.

Next day, 22 June, the battered canoe proceeded downstream, Mackay and one Indian guide paddling ahead in a smaller craft. Meeting a band of sixteen men and several women, Mackenzie was surprised to hear one of the women pronounce a few words in the Cree language. She had been taken prisoner by a party of Cree raiders from over the Rockies and, contriving to escape, had tried to rejoin her own tribe but, after all her hardships, had fallen into the hands of this band, who had driven her relations from the river into the mountains. Of her present husband she had no cause to complain, but she had a strong desire to return to her own people.

In the village were several Indians from farther downstream and one from the aest, perhaps a Sekani. The latter was completely intelligible to our party's interpreters. This, then, was a golden opportunity for Mackenzie to verify and extend his geographical information. It is thought that he was now at the site of Fort Alexandria, later to be built, and situated some thirty-five miles south of present-day Quesnel. It is important that we mentally locate this stopping point because here he was faced with a very difficult decision the results of which we shall consider in due course.

One of the Indians from farther downstream, most likely a Shuswap, drew, at Mackenzie's request, a sketch of the country on a large piece of bark, appealing to those who stood round, for confirmation or advice. He described the river itself as encumbered with falls and rapids, six of them impassable. The portages were of great length, passing over the cliffs and mountains. He knew the country of three successive tribes but beyond that it was still a long route to the sea about which he knew nothing. He had heard there was a lake before they reached the ocean, from which the natives did not drink.

Perhaps the 'lake' was the Gulf of Georgia and the ocean the true Pacific west of Vancouver Island. The wooden houses being built by white men, of which Mackenzie had heard the day before, had some reference to a trading settlement in Nootka Sound. One very old man said, that as long as he could remember, he had heard tell of white people to the southward and that one of them, according to tradition, had tried unsuccessfully to ascend the Fraser. To what possible Spanish trade or expedition this refers no one knows.

Amid all this vagueness and discouragement, one piece of information, which seemed reliable, must have stood out sharply. The Indians described, with circumstantial detail, a short route to the ocean, overland. The road, they said, was not difficult; it skirted the mountains, keeping to the low land, much of which was not forested. It took only six nights to reach the tribe from whom, in return for their furs and leather, they obtained iron, brass, copper, beads, etc. These goods were said to come from white men who were building houses two nights' journey farther on.

There was a thunder-storm, with heavy rain. When it passed, in the evening there was singing and dancing, the younger Indian women joining in. Mackenzie was filled with anxious thoughts and slept little that night. He must decide now whether to continue down river or strike overland to the coast.

Next morning, 23 June, after a further attempt to get information from the band, he made his decision. The pros and cons were fairly evenly balanced. Now that we have the advantage of knowing how much of his information was correct and how much misleading, we can see that his decision was for the best. If he continued downstream he would face canyons where portages were extremely difficult if not impossible, for who could lift canoes and goods up perpendicular cliffs? And all accounts agreed that the stream itself ran with such violence through rapids and over cataracts as to promise nothing but destruction. He had provisions for thirty days, over and above what his hunters or the natives might supply; his experience so far was that neither were dependable sources. He had a hundred and fifty bullets and about thirty pounds of shot: too little for safety. As he had descended the river to this point, the natives had become more numerous, more hostile and harder to communicate with. He made some word lists, as best he could, and it was clear that the visitors from downstream had a vocabulary of their own unlike anything so far encountered. How, in any case, could he negotiate with the natives from the bottom of a canyon carrying a roaring river? And, as it was flowing south rather than west, it must take a long course to the sea, a course that he would have first to follow, then to retrace against the force of the rapid current.

As he began his questioning that morning, one of the Indians asked why he needed to make such inquiries about their country. 'Do not you white men know every thing in the world?' It was a searching question and Mackenzie, after some thought, replied that his people 'were acquainted with the principal circumstances of every part of the world; that I knew where the sea is, and where I myself then was, but that I did not exactly understand what obstacles might interrupt me in getting to it; with which he and his relations must be well acquainted, as they had so frequently surmounted them.' It was a wise reply, recognizing the values of two kinds of knowledge.

Weighing the alternatives, he decided to retrace his course upriver to the point from which he could most conveniently strike overland toward the Pacific. Not even his sagacity could tell him that the Indians had grossly underestimated the distance. And he had no way of knowing that his reasoning about the Fraser was distorted by a simple lack of information. It seems probable that he assumed, from the sheer size and strength of the current, that this must be the River of the West and it is quite likely that he knew, from Spanish sources, of the mouth of a great stream—the Columbia—at about latitude 46°. It is just possible that he had heard of the exploration of the mouth of the Columbia, in 1792, by Captain Gray of Boston, from whose vessel the river takes its name.

He could not know and he had no reason to conjecture that the precipitation on this part of the Pacific slope supplied not one but two great rivers, and that the Fraser reached the sea just north of latitude 49°. He could only guess that the Fraser continued to flow roughly south, or on a twisting course, until it entered the Pacific too far from his present position to be of any use to him.

Once again, as leader, Mackenzie had to convince his followers that what he was proposing could be accomplished. After praising their fortitude, patience and perseverance, he explained his preference for the overland route. What he then added throws a flood of light on his character, temperament and tradition. 'I declared my resolution not to attempt it, unless they would engage, if we could not after all proceed over land, to return with me, and continue our voyage to the discharge of the waters, whatever the distance might be. At all events, I declared, in the most solemn manner, that I would not abandon my design of reaching the sea, if I made the attempt alone, and that I did not despair of returning in safety to my friends.' The men replied they would follow him wherever he should go.

To break out of their present circumstances, however, was easier said than done. As they prepared to embark, their guide insisted that he would go on foot back to his house and meet them there. Mackenzie was obliged to let him have his way but sent Mackay and two Indians with him. Next morning, 24 June, near the rendezvous, Mackay and the two Indians appeared, in a state of great alarm and without the guide. They had met a party of local Indians who had bows and arrows at the ready and seemed in a state of extreme rage. After a night in the woods, cold, wet and hungry, not daring to light a fire, the guide had left them abruptly. They had looked in vain for their friends at the rendezvous and concluded they had all been killed. So great was their demoralization that a general panic followed and everyone but Mackenzie was for abandoning the voyage as hopeless and impracticable. He alone remained firm. He was not afraid of the Indians, only of failing to complete his mission.

'I could not reflect on the possibility of such a disappointment but with sensations little short of agony.'

At this point an Indian came downstream in a canoe, landed and looked at the huts. To one of Mackenzie's Indians who went to speak to him he said his band would come and kill them all. Mackenzie made camp in a ruined house by the water, mooring the canoe so that in case of attack they had only to embark and push off. They passed a wretched night. A smouldering fire was kept, to repel the swarms of flies, but they did not dare make a blaze. Mackenzie, Mackay and three boatmen kept alternate watch and a sentinel, relieved every hour, kept additional watch nearby. Showers of rain fell during the night. Mackenzie arose at five. He was determined to return to their camp of the previous night and make another attempt to secure guides.

During the whole of this day, 25 June, and the next day, he made one effort after another to speak to Indians. On the advice of an old blind man, he moved again upstream, hoping to find bark and cedar wood to build a new canoe. His men were extremely dispirited and ready to give up the voyage as hopeless.

On 27 June they made camp in a clear space on a small island, near a stand of spruce. Early next morning, parties went out looking for suitable wood, watape (roots for sewing) and gum. The men, quite discouraged, were more willing to eat than to work and the man in charge of building the canoe, although skilful at the job, made no effort to push it forward. Choosing a time when the whole group were within earshot, Mackenzie reproached him, and indirectly the rest, saying they must make up their minds to follow him or not. He would go forward alone, if he had to. The work went on.

At this juncture who should appear but their guide, coming up in a canoe with a companion. He apologized for running off, explained he had been looking for his family and made it appear that all signs of hostility had arisen out of false reports that Mackenzie was unfriendly. This new aspect of affairs cheered the whole party and some forty-eight hours later, 1 July, the new canoe was ready for service. She was a stronger and better craft than the old one, though they had been obliged to reclaim gum from the latter, as so little was obtainable locally.

Next morning at half past three they were ready to leave. It had rained during the night; they had been cruelly bitten by sand-flies which Mackenzie thought must be 'the most tormenting insect of its size in nature'; they had been living on two meals a day, 'a regulation peculiarly offensive to a Canadian voyager'. But Mackenzie, from his diminishing supply, produced a dram of rum all round and, striking their paddles into the Fraser once more, they were 'in high spirits, when they perceived the superior excellence of the new vessel, and reflected that it was the work of their own hands'.

Next day, 3 July, they came to a small tributary which seemed to be the one they had heard of from the natives as leading toward the sea. Mackenzie named it West-Road River but their guide, whom they had expected to meet here, was not to be seen and they continued up the Fraser, hoping to find him. With six relations, he finally appeared resplendent in a beaver robe, and advised them not to return to West-Road River but to cut across country and strike the trail higher up.

By noon the next day, they had carefully buried a ninety-pound bag of pemmican, two bags of wild rice and a gallon keg of gunpowder and, for safety in another place, two bags of Indian corn and a bale of merchandise. Everything was rolled in a double layer of oil cloth and leather. The canoe was carefully stored on a platform, bottom up, and covered with branches, to keep the sun off. A hollow square of logs was built, ten feet by five, to contain all the tackle they could not carry.

What had to be carried was calculated with great care. Each of the voyageurs had a pack of about ninety pounds, a gun and ammunition. The Indians similarly, except that their packs were half the weight; even so 'they were very much dissatisfied, and if they had dared would have instantly left us. They had hitherto been very much indulged, but the moment was now arrived when indulgence was no longer practicable.' Mackenzie and Mackay carried about seventy pounds apiece, besides arms and ammunition, and across Mackenzie's shoulder swung the tube of his telescope, an awkward thing to carry in the bush. The path was well-beaten but the country rugged and heavily forested. They covered twelve miles that day.

During the next ten days the party plodded on, often cold and wet, never able to keep a reliable guide and, for sheer lack of time to hunt or fish, steadily running short of food. Their rations were cut by a third. They left the valley of the West-Road River and struggled over divides, finally reaching a stream, now known as Dean River, which flows west.

On 15 July a small group of Carrier Indians appeared, also heading for the coast. They gave Mackenzie some fish and said that, though they moved slowly because of their women and children, if he cared to stay with them the whole party would reach the coast in about three days. It was glad news to Mackenzie's exhausted men.

All the Carriers, even the children, were carrying packs of furs—beaver, otter, marten, lynx, bear—and of dressed leather. The coast Indians, they explained, in turn bartered the furs to white men who came in large canoes.

The next day, Mackenzie left two men behind to bury

secretly, under the place where their fire had been made, twenty pounds of pemmican. He was greatly concerned about food and increasingly so as he discovered that the Carriers had now decided to change their route for a somewhat longer one and his party must go on alone. Out of kindness, one of the Carriers offered to boil a kettle of fish roes for them, an operation which Mackenzie watched with growing misgiving. The dried roes were bruised between two stones, soaked in water, squeezed into a paste, boiled in a bark vessel by means of heated stones and seasoned with a pint of fish oil. Mackenzie had eaten roes before, thickened with meal, but the oil sickened him and he could not touch this curious dish. His men were either hungrier or less fastidious and ate it up.

Next day they went through a pass, walking on hard, drifted snow, directed by local Indians who told them that the river flowing into salt water, which they were seeking, was not far off. A storm of hail, snow and rain drove them for shelter to leeward of a huge rock. The hunters now brought in a small caribou but at this altitude and in this exposed position only a few crowberry bushes, not yet in blossom, and some stunted willows could be seen. Shivering they plodded on and in due course found wood, roasted their meat and were able to shave and change their clothes beside the comfort of a fire.

Ahead of them was a peak in the Coast Range, now known as Stupendous Mountain, from Mackenzie's own phrase: 'Before us appeared a stupendous mountain, whose snow-clad summit was lost in the clouds; between it and our immediate course flowed the river to which we were going.' Into the valley, which opened to their view as they went on, they began to descend, by a series of precipices covered with pine, spruce, hemlock, birch and other trees, their great size testifying to the rainfall. As they came down to the floor of the valley, cedars and alders appeared, larger than any Mackenzie had ever seen. He was in a quite different climate now and the berries on the bushes were ripe.

As darkness fell, their guides having gone ahead, they were obliged to feel their way through the dense woods but Mackenzie was determined to push on toward a village they had seen from above. At last they reached it and were soon being entertained, with fine hospitality, in a great house, raised on posts and reached by a broad timber cut with steps. Mats were placed before Mackenzie and Mackay and each was given a roasted salmon. The men received half a salmon each. To avoid inconvenience to his hosts, Mackenzie decided to sleep with his men outside. A fire was lit for them and boards placed for them to lie on. Two large dishes of creamed salmon roes flavoured with fruit and herbs were produced. Amid this warmth of hospitality, Mackenzie relaxed. 'I never enjoyed a more sound and refreshing rest, though I had a board for my bed, and a billet for my pillow.' The Indians were Bella Coolas.

In the morning, he was shown a weir which had been built into the river to lead the salmon into traps. It was ingeniously constructed and a great deal of labour had gone into laying down the alternate rows of logs and layers of gravel of which it was composed. The salmon and all that concerned taking them were regarded with great reverence. With meat the natives would have nothing to do, saying that the salmon would smell it and abandon them. Mackenzie's men had some caribou meat with them. A dog who swallowed a bit of the bone was beaten till he disgorged it. Another bone was thrown into the river, only to be retrieved by a native, who dived in, brought it out and burned it, then washed his hands to remove all taint.

On the western side of the Rockies Mackenzie had not hitherto been encountering insuperable difficulty with language. The Indians had been Athapascan speakers, the more important tribes located roughly as follows: Sekani, in the drainage basin of the upper Peace; Carrier, west of these, but not extending to the coast; Chilcotin, on the plateau west of the Fraser River. They differed, as we have seen, from the eastern Athapascan speakers on the other side of the mountains by their use of salmon, which they took from the upper reaches of the rivers. Their political and social structure was much the same as that on the eastern side of the Rockies.

The Bella Coolas were in every respect a new and strange experience for Mackenzie. Their language belonged to the Salish group of dialects, so that communication was very difficult. Though related to some Interior peoples, the Bella Coolas had long been isolated in a set of villages hemmed in by mountains and were hindered from coastwise movement by rocky shores and tortuous winding inlets. Their easy access to an abundant supply of salmon and the mild climate, in which heavy rains produced great stands of cedar, combined to encourage a sedentary village life. An elaborate mythology, an intense concern over the inheritance of ancestral names, a surprising skill in the carving of heraldic or totemic figures in wood: such essentials of Bella Coola tribal life have occupied and puzzled anthropologists.

These coast Indians appeared to Mackenzie more heavily built and better looking than the interior tribes; they seemed quieter and more peaceable. The men wore a single garment made of cedar bark finely divided, sometimes interwoven with strips of sea otter skin, and their hair was coated with oil and red earth.

At noon Mackenzie took an observation which gave 52° 28′ 11″ North latitude. Since the voyage began he had taken dozens of observations for latitude or longitude, often under very difficult conditions. Sometimes the terrain itself had defeated him, when he could establish no horizon, and once he had forgotten to wind his chronometer.

At one o'clock they embarked with their small baggage in two canoes, accompanied by seven of the natives, whose skill in handling their craft surpassed even that of the voyageurs themselves.

After two and a half hours they landed and came on foot to a village where, after a tumultuous reception, they were led to a house, larger and better built than anything they had yet seen. Here they were fed on roasted salmon and, as a great delicacy, cakes made of the dried inner rind of the hemlock tree which their hosts soaked in water, shredded and sprinkled with sweet oil.

The habits and customs of these Bella Coolas aroused Mackenzie's interest; he recognized that he was in the midst of a culture quite unknown to Canadian fur traders. The salmon were running and two Indians, out fishing, came in with their large canoe filled; some of the fish weighed as much as forty pounds. Unfortunately, Mackenzie had no one with him who could speak the language of the Bella Coolas, but many things can be understood through signs and it was clear that not even his kettle could be dipped in the river for fear of disturbing the fish, who 'dislike the smell of iron'.

Some of the dwellings, sheathed with boards and bark, were over a hundred feet long and forty feet in breadth. Each could contain several hearths; for partitions cedar planks were employed. The smoke found its way out through holes near the ridge pole and light came in the same way.

Painted figures on cedar panels and poles carved with animal crests or totems met Mackenzie's eye. Admiring the

Bella Coola River
Valley
H. D. von Tiesenhausen

'The Governor of Red River, Hudson's Bay, Voyaging in a Light Canoe 1824', by Peter Rindisbacher

The Public Archives of Canada

skill of these red and black formalized shapes and 'hiero-glyphics', he assumed they had a religious significance.

Though they had an abundant and assured food supply, from their position on a salmon river, and although, in building, weaving and carving, they seemed to show civilized skill unknown to the hunting peoples, yet in some matters these coast Indians were merely barbarous. One of the chief's sons was dying of malignant ulcers and Mackenzie was asked to give him some medicine. The native doctors were blowing on him, whistling, poking his stomach, putting their fingers into his mouth and spouting water through their lips into his face. They ended by carrying him into the woods, lighting a fire, and scarifying and cauterizing his ulcer so that Macken-zie, unable to bear the sight, had to leave.

In this village there were many signs of trade with white men. Spear points, arrow heads and personal ornaments were often of brass or copper. There was bar iron to make axes. There were poniards and daggers, some with Spanish coins inlaid in their handles.

When Mackenzie produced his sextant to take an altitude, he was warned not to do so and finally understood that the salmon would be frightened and might leave the river. As one would expect, he managed, nevertheless, to determine his latitude as 52° 25' 52". It was clear, also, that he was approaching salt water. By signs he was told that, about ten winters ago, the chief and forty of his people had taken the great cedar canoe—painted black, decorated with white figures of fish and inlaid on the gunwales with sea-otter teeth —and had paddled off toward the midday sun. They had seen two large vessels filled with men like Mackenzie, who received them kindly. These ships were quite likely Captain Cook's *Resolution* and *Discovery*.

Cook had lost his life in the Hawaiian Islands in a dispute

over a theft. A similar situation, common to many explorations, now confronted Mackenzie. As his party was about to leave the village, one of their axes was missing. Mackenzie appealed to the chief, who would not understand him. He then sat on a stone, with his gun, and made it appear that he would stay there till the axe returned. The village went into an uproar and it seemed possible the party would be attacked. The axe, however, appeared from under the chief's canoe and they left soon afterwards in a large craft with four of the village Indians. Mackenzie's comment on the lost axe is illuminating. 'Though this instrument was not in itself of sufficient value to justify a dispute with these people, I apprehended that the suffering them to keep it, after we had declared its loss, might have occasioned the loss of every thing we carried with us, and of our lives also. My people were dissatisfied with me at the moment; but I thought myself right then, and I think now, that the circumstances in which we were involved, justified the measure which I adopted.'

They went down the rapid current, stopping at some settlements and being obliged to shoot a cascade, and in the evening reached a village near the mouth of the river on the south bank. They ate the remains of their last meal, as no fish could be got from the natives in this place, and they slept in an empty house.

Next morning, 20 July, after some trouble about guides, they got off at an early hour and, about eight o'clock, reached salt water from the Pacific. They saw great numbers of 'sea-otters', perhaps seals, which eluded their bullets by the speed with which they dived. They saw gulls and porpoises.

Mackenzie was now in the same quandary he had been, for slightly different reasons, when he had reached the Arctic. Then he was a little unsure of his position, for lack of navigational instruments; now he was better equipped but, among these mountains and clouds, he might have difficulty in seeing the horizon and in finding a clear sky when he wanted it. In the Arctic, he had been in an estuary, not the open sea, but reasoned that no end would be served by his going further. Here he was at the end of a fiord, now known as North Bentinck Arm, and, considering the uncertainty of his relation with the local Indians and his dwindling stock of food, he knew he must begin the return journey with the least possible delay.

A young Indian, brother to the chief's son they had left so desperately ill, had accompanied the party down to this point. He was now eager to return: the swell was high, the wind boisterous, the canoe leaking. Mackenzie agreed that he should go and promised that he would himself return to the village in three nights.

Mackenzie's anxiety at this time was well founded. 'I had flattered myself with the hope of getting a distance of the moon and stars, but the cloudy weather continually disappointed me, and I began to fear that I should fail in this important object; particularly as our provisions were at a very low ebb, and we had as yet no reason to expect any assistance from the natives. Our stock was, at this time, reduced to twenty pounds weight of pemmican, fifteen pounds of rice, and six pounds of flour, among ten half-starved men, in a leaky vessel and on a barbarous coast.'

The barbarity which he had begun to sense was in part attributable, it is said, to the practices of white traders who came, in their ships, to secure beaver, sealskin and, particularly, sea-otter to be sold in China. Whereas the fur traders from Hudson's Bay or Canada were well aware of their utter dependence on co-operation from the Indians and made every effort to secure their goodwill, the captains of vessels on the Pacific were often little better than pirates and mixed fraud and violence with barter, careless of the future and concerned only to make a killing. The natives responded in kind and there were drownings and bloodshed.

Next day, 21 July, they met three canoes with fifteen men in them. They were Bella Bellas, who neighboured the Bella Coolas, though their language was different. One of them, with an insolent air, said that a large canoe, with white men in it, had recently been in that bay. A white man, Macubah, had fired on him and his friends, and another, Bensins, had struck him on the back with the flat of his sword. The names sound like Vancouver and Menzies—a naturalist who was with him. Vancouver's log shows he was in this fiord (Dean Channel) the previous month but records only his efforts to get in touch with the natives by every possible means, though in vain, because of their timidity. Mackenzie, knowing nothing of all this but with a strong distaste for the objectionable Bella Bella, concluded, 'I do not doubt but he well deserved the treatment which he described. He also produced several European articles, which could not have been long in his possession. From his conduct and appearance, I wished very much to be rid of him.' The man, however, forced himself into their canoe and asked to be taken to a narrow channel on the opposite shore, which he pointed to, saying it led to his village. They landed at the mouth of the channel, now known as Elcho Harbour, near some sheds which looked from a distance as though they might have been built by Europeans. It was only a ruined village but beside it a great rock stood up, which had clearly been used as a refuge or strongpoint and on the top of this Mackenzie camped. The natives, having harassed the party somewhat, went off near sunset with several stolen articles. Then another canoe arrived carrying seven men, with a sea-otter skin and a beautifully white skin, probably of a mountain goat. Mackenzie tried to barter for the former and for a seal they had just killed but without success. A scanty supper was eaten round a fire and throughout the cool, moonlight night the party kept a double watch in case of danger.

Mackenzie's precautions were not unwarranted. The Bella Bella had been culturally influenced by the Kwakiutl, a coastal people whose secret societies, elaborate masks and dramatic ceremonies are well known. A cultural trait among leading men of the Bella Bella was an aggressive arrogance. Mackenzie, ignorant of all these facts, must nevertheless have sensed the situation and decided to take a bold and wary attitude toward those who harassed him.

Soon after eight in the morning, Mackenzie made five observations to determine his longitude. Two canoes now arrived and some pieces of seal's flesh were obtained at a high price. At this point Mackay happened to light a piece of touch-wood with a burning glass, amazing the newcomers, who offered him the best of their otter skins for it. Two more canoes appeared and the young Indian who had come with them from upriver entreated Mackenzie to leave. They would soon gather to shoot their arrows and hurl their spears, he said. He was extremely anxious and foamed at the mouth. Mackenzie's own men, panic-stricken, asked if he intended to sacrifice them all. He replied that he had to complete his observations but that they should load the canoe, for instant departure. His task was almost done and he wished to leave a sign for any who might follow him or come in by sea. 'I now mixed up some vermilion in melted grease, and inscribed, in large characters, on the South-East face of the rock on which we had slept last night, this brief memorial—"Alexander Mackenzie, from Canada, by land, the twenty-second of July, one thousand seven hundred and ninety-three".'

The observations were still unfinished but, as a precaution against attack, they paddled three miles to reach a small cove on a point in what is now Dean Channel, where they could only be approached from one direction and could most readily defend themselves.

They were in one of the many long arms of the Pacific which, on this slowly sinking coast, reproduce all the features of a Norwegian fiord. The water was very deep, though the sounding line Mackenzie had hoped to plumb it with had just been stolen. The shores were of solid rock, rising from three to five hundred feet above high water mark. In odd pockets of soil grew cedar, spruce, birch and other trees, far larger than similar species in the mountains. Down the precipices threaded streams of clear and intensely cold water.

The local Indians followed, in two canoes, and tried to lure the young chief away. Mackenzie prevented this, for fear he might come to some harm or return alone to his father's village. It is extremely revealing to find that, in this difficult situation, none of the men would take any responsibility for the young chief's safekeeping. Mackenzie was obliged, in the midst of his other preoccupations, to keep watch over any attempt to escape. It is clear, however, that apart from removing him, when they first arrived, from one of the village canoes, Mackenzie used no force. Nor did he use threats. As usual, he was balancing all the elements of the situation against one another. 'I thought it much better to incur his displeasure, than to suffer him to expose himself to any untoward accident.'

In the afternoon, Mackenzie took five more altitudes, and observed the 'emersion' of Jupiter's first and third satellites. He reckoned his longitude as 128° 2′ 0″ West of Greenwich. 'I had now determined my situation, which is the most fortunate circumstance of my long, painful, and perilous journey, as a few cloudy days would have prevented me from ascertaining the final longitude of it.' As soon as this was done, they left, the men being very anxious to escape from the neighbourhood of these Indians. The tide was running out strongly but, by keeping close to the rock and working hard at their paddles, they made good progress.

They paddled all night, watching the Indian fires on shore, and at four thirty in the morning reached their camp of 20 July. The tide was low and they were obliged to land a mile below the village. Their guide was in great haste and Mackenzie, while his men were drawing the canoe above the reach of the tide, set off after him toward the village. When they came out of the bush and were within sight of the houses, two men suddenly rushed upon Mackenzie, furiously brandishing daggers. He presented his gun and, as they let the daggers drop, fastened to their wrists by a string, he let his gun fall into his left hand and drew his hanger (a short, curved sword). Other Indians appeared, armed with knives, and among them Mackenzie recognized the fellow who had already made so much trouble. He repeated the names Macubah and Bensins and made signs that they had shot at him. For once, Mackenzie became angry. 'Until I saw him my mind was undisturbed; but the moment he appeared, conceiving that he was the cause of my present perilous situation, my resentment predominated, and, if he had come within my reach, I verily believe, that I should have terminated his insolence forever.' He was indeed in peril. The Indians closed round him and one seized him from behind. Mackenzie shook him off but was still surrounded and outnumbered when one of his men came out of the wood.

The Indians withdrew. Within ten minutes, Mackenzie's whole party came in, one after another. Realizing that most of the gang who had harried them while they encamped on the rock were now in this village, he determined to get back his property and also his hat and cloak which had just been carried off. With their guns primed and ready, the party drew up in front of the house his assailants had retreated into and made signs that someone should come out. At last the young chief appeared, and told them the men in the canoes had spread the story that Mackenzie had ill-treated him and killed four others. This latter was so clearly untrue that the story of violence by Vancouver, which does not square with what we know of his stay in Dean Channel, was probably another fabrication.

Mackenzie explained the falsehood of the accusations, insisting that he be given his stolen articles and a few fish for his immediate needs. The young chief, whose actions are hard to explain, now appeared terrified and left for home, telling them to bring his father's canoes as they followed. In the midst of all this, Mackenzie, true to form, took an altitude and arrived at 52° 23' 43" North latitude. He named the place Rascal's Village.

Mackenzie's men now went through a spasm of complete demoralization. Knowing that the troublemaker and some of his friends had gone upstream in a canoe, they concluded that, at the next village, they would be in worse danger than ever, especially as the young chief would probably give a bad account of things to his father. With the exception of Mackay, who always gave his leader steady support, they were in a state of rebellion, determined to abandon the canoe, bypass the village and walk over the mountains toward home. They began throwing into the river anything they thought they could not carry on their backs.

Sitting on a stone, Mackenzie waited for this wave of unreasoning terror to subside, but at last began putting his own argument to them. They would be out of food within two days, if they left the river, and, if they climbed the ranges, they would perish of cold. Furthermore, one of their own Indians was sick and could not walk; they must not abandon him. Having reached his goal, he, as leader, was now concerned only with what concerned them—how to return, with the least danger and as quickly as possible, to their starting point. The steersman, who had been with Mackenzie for five years, said he would follow him wherever he went. Reason slowly began to reassert itself. The party resumed their journey upstream, some on foot, some in the canoe. The current was very strong and the canoe had to be dragged by overhanging branches. Mackay's gun was swept overboard and lost.

They came in sight of the first house and saw the young chief, with six others, coming in a canoe to meet them. This was a good sign and, landing, they found a welcome and procured some fish. At the next house, which the canoe reached as darkness fell, the turbulent Indian and four companions appeared. They had not stirred up trouble here, however, perhaps because they were on business; it turned out they were traders from the seaward islands, offering cedar bark ready to weave, fishspawn, copper, iron and beads, in exchange for roasted salmon, hemlock-bark cakes, salmon roe, sorrel and berries. Their canoe was full of boxes.

The party passed a quiet night, but found in the morning that the young chief had gone off upstream with their canoe. Two of the local Indians, however, agreed to come with them in another canoe and on the next day, 25 July, reached the Great Village, as Mackenzie decided to name it. He approached it with great caution. Leaving Mackay and the men at the river bank, he walked to the chief's house without a gun but with his pistols in his belt. If they heard these fired, they would know he was being attacked and act accordingly.

He was uncertain where to go because there were several paths and two great wings, already hung thickly with salmon, had been added to the chief's house. Some women were supping on salmon roes and berries and invited him to join them. All seemed peaceful, yet Mackenzie's instinct was not at fault. The old chief with his son, who had been the guide, appeared. The old man's hair was cut off and his face blackened. In his hand was a beaded tobacco pouch which the son had purloined from Mackay. He threw this at Mackenzie with great indignation and walked off. He was evidently very angry or very much disturbed. Mackenzie immediately greeted the son, who had recently deserted them, in a friendly way, taking him by the hand. Mackay had just appeared, showing signs of alarm and bringing Mackenzie's hanger. They joined the old chief, who at last explained himself.

His son who had suffered from the ulcers was dead. He had been in great anxiety about the other son, afraid that Mackenzie's men had killed him or that the whole party had perished together. Taking father and son by the hands, Mackenzie led them back to his own people, who rejoiced to see them, and from his dwindled stock of goods gave them knives, cloth, and indeed something of everything he still possessed. This had the effect of restoring him to the chief's favour, but he sensed it was all very precarious—'these people are of so changeable a nature, that there is no security with them'.

The party now left the village, Mackay in the lead, the men in Indian file at a steady pace and Mackenzie in the rear for fear of further trouble. The people of the village could be heard disputing, whether to stop them or not, but the whole party got clear. Their path led through a forest of stately cedars and, for a good omen, their dog appeared and they felt 'the sensation of having found a lost friend'. He was reduced almost to a skeleton, from lack of food, and seemed half demented, approaching them, then running away. He had been scavenging in one of the villages and probably by now expected always to be driven off. As they went on, they dropped a little food for him and gradually he rejoined them and became his old self.

That night they did not venture to make a fire but each man lay down beneath his own tree, in his clothes and with his arms beside him. The night passed undisturbed.

In the morning, 26 July, they set out at daybreak and arrived by eight at the first of the riparian villages they had reached on the outward journey. They were now referring to it as Friendly Village and, as they expected, were received with great kindness. The chief, taking them into his house, showed every hospitality. Mackenzie presented him with two yards of blue cloth (which had been carried so many hundred miles), an axe, knives and other articles. In turn the chief offered a large shell of mother-of-pearl, which his people used to make bracelets and ear-rings. He had no sea-otter skins but promised to have a good supply if Mackenzie or his friends should return by sea. It was a peaceful and pleasant village, with no lack of food and shelter. In the interval between Mackenzie's two visits, five more houses had been built and were seen thickly hung with salmon. The women were busy boiling salmon roe, mixed with sorrel or berries, in large square kettles of cedar wood. This was poured, when cooked, into wooden frames and left in the sun to form dried cakes. Mackenzie's keen eye noted many things of interest: the prevailing wedge-shaped head was artificially induced by being closed in leather-covered boards while the child was carried over the shoulder in a frame fixed on a wooden backing. He had not seen this kind of cradle elsewhere. The planks and timbers for the houses were made with a hatchet, a mallet and a wooden wedge. 'They must also have other tools with which they complete and polish their work, but my stay was so short, my anxiety so great, and my situation so critical, that many circumstances may be supposed to have escaped me.'

At eleven they left this place, well deserving the name of Friendly Village, and were accompanied for about a mile by all the men belonging to it, who seemed to regret their leaving. The mountains were before them and after fording a fork of the river, they began to climb the precipices. The sick Indian, though somewhat recovered, was still weak, and Mackenzie, with some difficulty, had carried him through a rapid current three feet deep. To find water and a camping place at the higher level, before night fell, they were forced to press on quickly, but two were left with the Indian, to bring him along at his own pace. After a continuous climb of over four hours, they camped but were so exhausted they could barely crawl about to gather wood for the fire. About seven the others appeared, relieving all anxiety.

They had left the coast region, with its salmon, its dug-out canoes, its sea-otter skins and huge cedars, thousands of feet below and were back where unmelted snow lay in drifts, where the grass was barely showing green and the crowberry bushes were just beginning to blossom. But their spirits rose with a sense of accomplishment. 'We consoled ourselves by sitting round a blazing fire, talking of past dangers, and indulging the delightful reflection that we were thus far advanced on our homeward journey. Nor was it possible to be in this situation without contemplating the wonders of it. Such was the depth of the precipices below, and the height of the mountains above, with the rude and wild magnificence of the scenery around, that I shall not attempt to describe such an astonishing and awful combination of objects; of which, indeed, no description can convey an adequate idea.'

They continued over the mountains for nine days, uneventfully. On Sunday, 4 August, they came back to the Fraser, having picked up their buried pemmican in good condition. There was a moment of real danger, when the party was threatened by a group of Indians they had not met before and who were alarmed at their approach to the lodges. But in the morning they found the canoe, its equipment and their buried goods, all in good order, with the exception of some cloth that had got wet. The provisions, of which they were now in great need, were unharmed. It was a comfort to have their tent again. A blazing fire was lit and Mackenzie served out a dram of rum to all, but they had been so long without any it seemed to have lost its relish.

That day they took things easily. Mackenzie made his usual observations. These gave the longitude as 53° 24' 10". Many natives arrived and, in return for large knives, fifteen beaver robes were secured. Now that they had their canoe again, the weight and bulk of what they picked up was no longer so sharply limited. Confident in the honesty of the local natives, Mackenzie's men did not guard their belongings and a number of articles were stolen. Surprised that the same people who had left their canoe and all its equipment untouched should now steal the cooking utensils, and anxious to avoid a quarrel, Mackenzie for once resorted to a piece of finesse. He gravely informed the Indians present that the white men controlled the ocean and, if his goods were not returned, no salmon would be permitted to come past the mouth of the river. Messengers were sent off to bring back everything stolen, several large salmon were then bought for supper, and a day of relative peace and fair weather ended with a delicious meal. Everything was in order for an early departure the next morning.

They were now back among Carriers, who had no fire-arms, only bows and arrows and spears. Their language was of the Athapascan group and easily intelligible. The strange world of the Pacific coast, with its different customs, alien languages, sedentary civilization and dug-out cedar canoes, was far behind now. The salmon, however, those intrepid travellers upstream, were still running strongly, even at this distance from the ocean, and in places the water seemed covered with their fins.

Day by day the homeward voyage continued and on 12 August they turned out of the stream of the Fraser into its tributary the McGregor. They were now re-encountering the dangers and fatigues of crossing the divide, but with some advantages: much of the snow on the higher slopes had melted and the water was in places six feet lower; they knew what they would encounter; and, although so exhausted and short of food that they were not as strong or resilient, they could foresee the end of the journey. The legs and feet of the whole party were quite benumbed; Mackenzie could walk only with great difficulty.

On the 16th, they reached the height of land that forms the actual divide. The next day, after a portage, because of drift wood in the stream, they reached the Parsnip. 'The meadow through which we passed was entirely inundated; and from the state of my foot and ancle, I was obliged, though with great reluctance, to submit to be carried over it.' At two in the afternoon, at the mouth of a small tributary, they found a package displayed to catch the eye. It was the four (originally mentioned as five) beaver skins left on the outward journey with the Indian who had given them to Mackenzie. For some reason he had taken this means of ensuring their delivery and, struck by his honesty, Mackenzie left three times their value in goods at the same spot.

On 20 August they came to the portage around Peace River Canyon, which Mackenzie calls Portage de la Montagne de Roche and which had given them so much trouble on the westward journey. Although Mackenzie seems to have been aware that the Indian portage, if longer, was easier, for some reason the party retraced their own painful footsteps. They had food enough for only two meals and were desperately anxious to find game. Mackay and the Indians were sent off to hunt, while the rest carried. At sunset, with the work of carrying half done, the hunters returned laden with buffalo meat. A hearty meal and the removal of all anxiety on the score of food made for a cheerful evening.

Next day, Mackenzie's ankle being almost well and the men in good spirits, the canoe was carried down the mountain and repaired, poles were cut and, after a chilly night at this altitude, they were ready to leave at seven in the morning of 22 August. At noon, having run several rapids, they arrived at a rendezvous agreed on with Mackay and the hunters, who had killed two elk and already roasted some choice cuts. After so long a period of intense labour on short commons, the men were ravenous. Another elk was sighted and killed that afternoon. 'To give some idea of our appetites, I shall state the elk, or at least the carcase of it, which we brought away, to have weighed two hundred and fifty pounds; and as we had taken a very hearty meal at one o'clock, it might naturally be supposed that we should not be very voracious at supper; nevertheless, a kettle full of the elk flesh was boiled and eaten, and that vessel replenished and put on the fire. All that remained, with the bones, &c. was placed, after the Indian fashion, round the fire to roast; and at ten next morning the whole was consumed by ten persons and a large dog, who was allowed his share of the banquet. This is no exaggeration; nor did any inconvenience result from what may be considered as an inordinate indulgence.'

Next morning, 23 August, they were on the water before daylight. The weather was warm. Great herds of buffalo appeared as they moved downstream. Food in abundance and their long voyage almost over.

The following day, warm weather continued and the country looked more and more beautiful as they descended the Peace. The Fort came into view. 'We threw out our flag, and accompanied it with a general discharge of our fire-arms.' In a burst of speed, the paddles flying, they drew up at the wharf before the two men they had left behind in the spring could so much as fire a welcoming shot. They landed at four in the afternoon.

'Here my voyages of discovery terminate. Their toils and their dangers, their solicitudes and sufferings, have not been exaggerated in my description. On the contrary, in many instances, language has failed me in the attempt to describe them. I received, however, the reward of my labours, for they were crowned with success.

'As I have now resumed the character of a trader, I shall not trouble my readers with any subsequent concern, but content myself with the closing information, that after an absence of eleven months, I arrived at Fort Chepewyan, where I remained, for the purposes of trade, during the succeeding winter.'

V

Montreal, London, Scotland

DURING the winter of 1793–4, at Fort Chipewyan, Mackenzie was feeling the effects of his strenuous westward journey.
Roderick had been sent to another post and in the letters
Alexander wrote to him we find an unusual degree of self-
revelation.

On 13 January, 1794, he writes that he wishes both of them
could get down to Grand Portage and he continues—though
one or two words are doubtful in the text—'I am fully bent
on going down. I am more anxious now than ever. For I
think it unpardonable in any man to remain in this country
who can afford to leave it. What a pretty situation I am in
this winter—starving and alone—without the power of doing
myself or any body else any Service. The Boy at Lac La
Loche or even my own Servant is equal to the performance
of my Winter Employment.'

In March he writes again to Roderick. He wishes he could
enclose with the letter a draft of his Journal which he had
hoped his cousin would look over and, if necessary, correct.
But he cannot do so. 'Last fall I was to begin copying it—but
the greatest part of my time was taken up in vain speculations
—I got into such a habit of thinking that I was often lost
in thoughts nor could I ever write to the purpose—what I
was thinking of—would often occur to me instead of what
which I ought to do—I never passed so much of my time
so insignificantly—nor so uneasy—Although I am not

superstitious—dreams amongst other things—caused me much annoyance I could not close my eyes without finding myself in company with the Dead—I had visions of late which almost convince me that I lost a near relation or a friend—It was the latter end of January when I began my work—thinking then I had time enough—though the reverse is the fact—and I will be satisfied and so must you, if I can finish the copy to give you reading of it in the Spring—I find it a work that will require more time than I was aware of—for it is not a quarter finished.'

In the spring he left Fort Chipewyan and went down to Grand Portage. He was never to see Athabasca, or indeed any part of the great western country, again. At the summer meeting of the North West partners, they were sufficiently appreciative of his achievement to give him another share and to make him one of the Company's agents. This meant that he would be posted in Montreal and it was clearly, so far as the 'wintering partners' were concerned, a move to protect their own interests. These men, who were assigned to posts in the north and west, represented the nerve endings of the system, in touch with the actualities of Indian trade, and they were alarmed when the intelligence they transmitted to the centre in Montreal met with no response. Mackenzie, one of themselves, would be their interpreter.

He had, however, more than this on his mind. As he journeyed, in the autumn, to the St Lawrence, he stopped at Niagara and went up to Navy Hall. This log building had housed naval officers during the War of American Independence and had been converted into an official residence for the first Lieutenant-Governor of Upper Canada, John Graves Simcoe, who had been installed three years earlier. Mackenzie, like Othere producing his walrus tooth for King Alfred, presented his Excellency with a sea-otter skin from the Pacific. He wrote a brief report which he amplified in conversation and, from a long report concerning the west which Simcoe sent to the British Government, we know what lines of action Mackenzie urged. Simcoe was much impressed by his visitor, whom he thought 'as intelligent as he is adventurous'. The cardinal points of Mackenzie's plan were, as one would expect, simple and practical. Rival interests in the western fur trade must be amalgamated. The government should take the initiative; to insure that control of western trade and territory remained with Britain, it should establish two posts on the Pacific coast. Goods should be supplied to this region through Hudson Bay or via Cape Horn. The actual trade with western tribes would be best handled by men drawn from Lower Canada; they understood the country and its Indians, which was not the case with the crews of seagoing vessels.

The maritime fur trade of the northern Pacific coast began when Vitus Bering found sea-otter off the coast of Alaska in 1741. The superb fur of the otter—a brown inner pile, soft and dense, overlaid by heavier gray-tipped hairs—made Chinese officials willing to pay enormous prices. A good pelt ultimately sold for over $2,000. Inevitably this unprotected resource invited plunder. By the end of the next century the sea-otter was nearly exterminated. Only a long policy of internationally enforced protection has at last permitted the re-establishment of herds to the point where limited taking of pelts is again being allowed.

The sea-otter was not the only one to suffer. Some ships' captains were little better than pirates. In return for brutal treatment, Coast Indians made a series of attacks upon ships, of which the *Tonquin* massacre was a spectacular example. The most successful traders were Americans, unhampered by British restrictions and closer to their home ports than

British captains. The harvest was a rich one, including such furs as beaver and marten, as well as sea-otter pelts and sealskins. Mackenzie's plan would have enabled the North-Westers to dominate and humanize this trade. They had an impressive record of good organization and fair dealing.

In Montreal, Mackenzie submitted a report to the Governor-General, Lord Dorchester. He went to London that winter, then returned to Montreal in the summer of 1795 and settled down to his duties as agent of the North West Company. Although he was perhaps the most prominent figure in the fur trade, his difficulties with his own company steadily increased. McTavish, the old veteran who had long managed to get his own way with the Company's policies, frankly disliked Mackenzie and had little sympathy with his scheme of expansion beyond the Rockies. The Company, moreover, had to cope with increasing competition.

In 1796 Britain finally lost control of all military posts south of the Great Lakes, including such important points as Detroit and Michilimackinac. The American government, moving in, reserved the trade in its own territory for American traders. This meant increased competition among Canadian traders for the furs of the north-west. Among new associations, the most vigorous was probably the XY Company, which proceeded in 1797 to establish a post at Grand Portage across the Pigeon River from the North West Company's buildings. They pushed their operations into the valleys of the Red River and the Assiniboine and were soon reaching right up into the Athabasca territory. They were able to cut into the profits of both North West and Hudson's Bay Companies, the latter having hopefully extended its operations further from salt water and into the interior. All the old evils of intense competition raised their heads again—

plots and counterplots, bribery of the Indians with liquor, rivalry ready to break into violence.

At the beginning of this period, Mackenzie was in a state of high prosperity. In 1795 the Beaver Club elected him to its prized membership. Established in 1785, it was at first limited to men who had spent a winter in the north-west. Its dinners were famous and a list of its members resembles a roll call of the great names of the fur trade.

About this time Mackenzie made a favourable impression upon the Duke of Kent who had been sent to Quebec in 1791 in command of the 7th Fusiliers. The two men had something in common, the Duke being a frustrated man of action and capable of energetic moves in emergencies. When Mackenzie was from time to time in England, he was repeatedly the Prince's travelling companion and his knighthood may have owed something to this connection.

Mackenzie and Duncan McGillivray, another North-Wester, gave a dinner in December, 1797, of which one of the guests, the army officer named George Thomas Landmann, has left the following account: 'In those days we dined at four o'clock, and after taking a satisfactory quantity of wine, perhaps a bottle each, the married men, viz. Sir John Johnson, McTavish, Frobisher, O'Brien, Judge Ogden, Tom Walker, and some others retired, leaving about a dozen to drink to their health. We now began in right earnest and true highland style, and by four o'clock in the morning, the whole of us had arrived at such a degree of perfection, that we could all give the war-whoop as well as Mackenzie and McGillivray, we could all sing admirably, we could all drink like fishes, and we all thought we could dance on the table without disturbing a single decanter, glass or plate by which it was profusely covered; but on making the experiment we discovered that it was a complete delusion, and ultimately, we broke all the plates, glasses, bottles, &c., and the table also, and worse than all the heads and hands of the party received many severe contusions, cuts and scratches.'

On 12 May, 1798, we find the young Landmann again in the company of the North-Westers. His account is both amusing and illuminating. 'At La Chine we found the two canoes destined to proceed with us, by the shore opposite to a house belonging to the North-West Company; and wherein an abundant luncheon was waiting our arrival. Several officers in the army, amongst them Colonel Gordon and Lieutenant McArthur, of the 60th regiment, and some of the North-West Company, not about to form part of our expedition, had accompanied us, all of them, I believe, natives of the Highlands of Scotland, so that I was the only *foreigner* amongst them. We sat down, and without loss of time expedited the lunch intended to supersede a dinner, during which time the bottle had freely circulated, raising the old Highland drinking propensity, so that there was no stopping it; Highland speeches and sayings, Highland reminiscences, and Highland farewells, with the dioch and dorich, over and over again, was kept up with extraordinary energy, so that by six or seven o'clock, I had, in common with many of the others fallen from my seat. To save my legs from being trampled on, I contrived to draw myself into the fire-place, and sat up in one of the corners there being no stove or grate. I there remained very passive, contemplating the proceedings of those who still remained at table, when at length Sir Alexander Mackenzie, as president, and McGillivray, as vice-president, were the last retaining their seats. Mackenzie now proposed to drink to our memory, and then give the war-whoop over us, fallen foes or friends, all nevertheless on the floor, and in attempting to push the bottle to McGillivray, at the opposite end of the table, he slid off his chair, and could not recover his seat whilst McGillivray, in extending himself over the table, in the hope of seizing the bottle which Mackenzie had attempted to push to him, also in like manner began to slide on one side, and fell helpless on the floor.'

Landmann had a great faculty for recalling adventures which furnish useful and detailed information. Let us follow him a little further.

'Early in the month of May 1799, I received an order to proceed again to the island of St Joseph; and having mentioned that circumstance to Sir Alexander Mackenzie and to Mr W. McGillivray, they very kindly offered me a passage in a canoe in which they were about to proceed by the St Lawrence to Kingston, Niagara, Detroit and Michilimakinac. . . . During the night we suffered severely from cold, the cause of which was readily explained, as soon as the daylight opened to our view the waters of Lake Erie (on the borders of which we were encamped), covered as far as we could see with packed ice. Notwithstanding this obstruction we put the canoe into the water, loaded it, and pushed off, when to my surprise, with some care, and by placing a paddle upright on each side of the bows to fend-off the ice, we very gently advanced, with setting poles forcing to the right and left as much of the floating ice as we could, so as to avoid injuring the canoe. In this manner we reached the clear surface through a distance of about four miles, and shortly afterwards arrived in a very comfortable warm atmosphere.'

They attempt to cross Saganaw Bay, in Lake Huron: 'After careful consideration, it was thought better to attempt crossing the bay at its mouth to the tedious navigation round its coast. The weather was exceedingly tranquil, the wind light from the eastward, and we still could depend on six or seven hours of daylight, which it was believed would be sufficient either to complete the *traverse*, or at least to gain a view of the land at the opposite point of the bay before night-fall. These circumstances had induced us to adopt the direct line across the mouth of the bay. Our men, fully aware of the importance of not waiting a moment, urged an immediate departure; and away we went in high spirits, every pipe filled and lighted, and the best singer in the canoe singing the very best canoe song, which the high cliff-like land at Point-aux-Barques re-echoed with fading voice as we advanced.

'Six and even seven hours had expired, yet no land could be seen ahead, and we had for some hours past lost sight of the Point-aux-Barques. The sun had descended below the horizon, and the young moon was making haste to follow his example, yet no land was visible in any direction. Our anxiety increased, and various were the speculations as to the failure of our calculations. Some thought we had overrated our speed, others that we had stood out too far to our right, and had actually passed the northern cape of the bay out of sight of land; there might be a current carrying us out of our course; and many other conjectures were set forth without profit. The light left us, and we had not seen any land, whilst the wind, right in our teeth, was rapidly increasing. In the midst of these conjectures, two hours after the sun had left us, the man in the bow with a terrific voice screamed out, "Breakers in every direction; stop the canoe!"

' "Stop her!" was the cry from every mouth at once; but our canoe was not a steamer, and the directions were more easily said than done. By the utmost efforts of the men, how-ever, we did stop, just in time to escape total wreck, for one touch on the angular rocks surrounding, would have done it. With setting poles pushed out in all directions, we contrived to retreat, and got out into water free from breakers, whither we thought it necessary to remain until daylight should come to our rescue.

'The long and anxiously-desired rising of the sun at length came, and we soon discovered that we had in the darkness of the night hit exactly on the only part of the coast where rocks could be found. Had we gone to the right or to the left but a few hundred yards, we should have effected a landing on a beautifully steep shore of hard sand, whereas we had arrived on the extremity of a long reef of detached blocks of stone.

'Notwithstanding the surf ran high, we found a tolerably sheltered spot and soon had a kettle on the fire.'

The air of prosperity and cameraderie which Landmann records was not, however, the whole story. Rivalry between Mackenzie and McTavish continued and when, in 1799, Mackenzie's contract with the Company expired, he did not sign on for a fresh term, though there is evidence that the men who actually wintered in the western posts, appreciating his first-hand knowledge of their difficulties, urged him to continue. Alexander Henry, a partner of the Company, whose uncle of the same name had also been a partner and who for that reason is usually referred to as 'the younger', left on record his opinion of the affair: 'The old North West Company is all in the hands of McTavish [and] Frobisher, and Mackenzie is out. The latter went off in a pet. The cause as far as I can learn was who should be the first—McTavish or Mackenzie, and as there could not be two Caesars in Rome, one must remove.'

As he went to England that autumn, we may assume that his prime disagreement with McTavish was over the tactics of western expansion and that he endeavoured to persuade the British government to establish its claim to the Pacific coast he had reached. It is likely that his friendship with the

Duke of Kent was of use to him at this time. In the spring of 1800 he was again in Montreal and probably active in organizing a company known as the New North West Company, also called the XY Company, a name that had already, as early as 1798, been applied to competitors of the old North West Company. Although the new XY Company was short of men who had first-hand knowledge of the north-west, it had a relatively large capital and Mackenzie may have hoped that it would rapidly penetrate the lands beyond the Rockies. What he was thinking and how many times he crossed the Atlantic in the two years before the publication of his *Voyages* are not easy to ascertain but it is evident that he was doing his utmost to persuade the British government to establish its authority on the Pacific margin.

The *Voyages*, which appeared in November, 1801, are intended, not only to tell the story of the two great journeys, but also to inform the reader about the fur trade, induce him to study the map of the northern half of North America and persuade him of opportunities for British commerce.

No one interested in Mackenzie can afford to miss the sentences in his Preface in which he frankly admits his limitations. He was an explorer whose aims had to be strictly concerned with the commercial organization he belonged to and he did not pretend to any further competence or to any wider objectives.

'These voyages will not, I fear, afford the variety that may be expected from them; and that which they offered to the eye, is not of a nature to be effectually transferred to the page . . . I could not stop to dig into the earth, over whose surface I was compelled to pass with rapid steps; nor could I turn aside to collect the plants which nature might have scattered on the way, when my thoughts were anxiously employed in making provision for the day that was passing over me. I had to encounter perils by land and perils by water; to watch the savage who was our guide, or to guard against those of his tribe who might meditate our destruction ... Today I had to assuage the rising discontents, and on the morrow, to cheer the fainting spirits of the people who accompanied me. The toil of our navigation was incessant, and oftentimes extreme; and in our progress over land, we had no protection from the severity of the elements, and possessed no accommodations or conveniences but such as could be contained in the burden on our shoulders, which aggravated the toils of our march, and added to the wearisomeness of our way.'

His readers are not to look for 'embellished narrative or animated description'. He describes what he has seen 'with the impressions of the moment which presented it to me'. He declines 'to wander into conjecture'; if he speaks confidently on any subject it is because his experience has given him special knowledge. 'I am not a candidate for literary fame; at the same time, I cannot but indulge the hope that this volume, with all its imperfections, will not be thought unworthy the attention of the scientific geographer; and that, by unfolding countries hitherto unexplored, and which, I presume, may now be considered as a part of the British dominions, it will be received as a faithful tribute to the prosperity of my country.'

His preface comes full circle. He is first, last and always a trader. 'Sono mercanti,' said Napoleon, picking up a phrase from Paoli to describe the British people. Mackenzie would have taken it as a compliment. In his way of thinking, to discover new lands and add them to Britain's commercial empire was an achievement to take pride in. If we compare this process to Napoleonic conquests and subjugations, we can perhaps recover a little of his glow of satisfaction.

Not content to make this general and public statement of his views, Mackenzie also submitted, early in 1802, a set of proposals to the Colonial Secretary, Lord Hobart.

He calls his memorandum 'Preliminaries to the Establishment of a permanent British Fishery and Trade in Furs, &c., on the Continent and West Coast of North America'. His first article is as follows: 'To form a supreme Civil and Military Establishment, on the centrally situated and Navally defensible Island of Nootka, at King George's Sound, Lat. 50° North. with two subordinates: one in the River Columbia, Lat. 46°, and the other on Sea Otter Harbour, Lat. 55° North.' He adds to this the following observation: 'Priority of occupation vesting sovereignty in the possessor, no time to be lost. Vide Treaty with Spain of 1790.'

What he had in mind is clear and straightforward. He wanted to clinch for Britain the possession of Vancouver Island and to establish claims to the coast as far to the north as the Russian sphere of influence and southward to the valley of the Columbia, a strip of coast about twelve hundred miles in length as the crow flies, though so deeply indented that the actual coastline is many times longer. His last point, concerning the treaty with Spain, was an important one. In 1789, the year of Mackenzie's trip to the Arctic, four British trading vessels in Nootka Sound had been seized by the Spaniards and the final settlement of the dispute that followed was in the form of a convention which left it open to either country to establish posts in places not already occupied. In 1795 the Spanish abandoned their settlement at Nootka, probably finding it too far from their Mexican bases, and Mackenzie saw it as a natural centre for Pacific trade. As Fraser did not descend the lower course of the river that bears his name until 1895, Mackenzie had no means of knowing that a site at or near its mouth would be preferable. His recommendation was sound in relation to all the geographical facts obtainable at that time.

The rest of the 'Preliminaries' which Mackenzie sent to Lord Hobart are concerned with the organization of trade. A principal obstacle to the free flow of commerce was the existence of privileged chartered companies, survivals of an earlier 'mercantile' age. The East India Company, for example, had a legal monopoly of British trade with China (which it did not lose until 1833). Mackenzie submitted that, if trans-Pacific trade was to flourish, ships flying the British flag must not be restricted in any way; a British captain must be able to carry furs direct to Canton, as freely as an American could. Nor must the Hudson's Bay Company restrict the passage of English merchandise to the Pacific Coast or the return passage of furs. On the positive side, Mackenzie's document recommended the foundation of a new company in London to be called 'The Fishery and Fur Company', in which the existing North West Company and XY Company would join with English partners who could supply fresh capital. Part of this new money would be used to acquire whaling vessels. 'The Whalers might carry out from England all the British articles Saleable or rather barterable for the furs and other Products of America, and bring back such part of the latter as would best suit the British Market; while other vessels of such a size and construction as may be found best adapted might be employed to carry the samples to Canton and such other Settlements of the East India Company as offer the best Market in the way either of Sale or Barter.'

Mackenzie's total concept was admirable in its simplicity, its comprehensiveness and its practicality. Had it been carried out, Britain would have been in a position to compete effectively with American traders in the Pacific. Unhappily,

neither part of his proposal was achieved. The British government, although it had signed the Peace of Amiens in March,
1802, was at war with France again in 1803 and Napoleon
had an invasion army massed at Boulogne. It was too much
to hope that ships and men could be found in Britain to set
up posts for the promotion of trade on the other side of the
world.

The other part of Mackenzie's plan, the union of the rival
fur trading groups into one grand company with fresh
capital, fared equally badly. He came back to Montreal, at
Lord Hobart's suggestion, to try to unite the North West and
XY Companies. But it was of no use and in October, 1802,
he writes to the under-secretary for the Colonies, enclosing
some documents. 'The papers', he writes, 'will explain themselves, and, I am sorry to say, show that I have not succeeded;
as also evince the improbability of my being able to succeed
in bringing about the union between the two Fur Companies,
which my Lord Hobart so strongly recommended to me as
the first step towards the accomplishment of my favourite
project; Without the aid of Government, by granting the
Licenses (I had the honour of proposing) to one of the con-
tending parties, with the condition that the other party
should have the option of sharing, in the proportion of the
Trade they might be carrying on, to that part of His
Majesty's Dominions, I see no means of bringing about a
coalition for several years to come, making the Western
Establishment lost perhaps for ever.'

His letter then goes on to urge, once again, the necessity of
'an immediate Military Establishment upon the Western
Coast of North America, so as to prevent other nations
anticipating us in an object the importance of which cannot
at present be foreseen in all its consequences'.

Although his plans fell through, he had no reason to complain of personal neglect. Early in 1802 he was knighted by George III and he began to enjoy the fame of a great explorer. His book was widely read. Within two years, three editions were needed in the United States and translations appeared in German and French.

Soon after the honour of knighthood was conferred, he paid a visit to his sisters in Scotland. In Ayr a grand ball was given in his honour. There was a large attendance of local gentry and Scottish pride in the exploits, success and honours achieved by a native son found full expression.

It was the same when, later in the year, he returned to Montreal. His achievements shone all the brighter from the burnishing they had received in Britain. In the Beaver Club he was lionized. The XY Company partners made him their head and were often referred to as 'Sir Alexander Mackenzie and Company'. He was elected, in 1804, to the Legislative Assembly of Quebec.

With his old partners in the North West Company, headed by Simon McTavish, he was now in bitter competition. The period 1802-4 witnessed a return to the cut-throat methods associated with the period of John Ross's murder, which had proved at that time to be intolerable and had been brought to an end by the merger of 1787. Now the bad old practices returned: the Indians were bribed with liquor; the beaver were overkilled. Still the companies failed to show a profit.

In July, 1804, the unexpected death in Montreal of Simon McTavish, at the age of fifty-four, changed the whole picture. Without delay, the two companies combined and a great surge of exploration and trade followed, in the history of which the names of two North West men, Simon Fraser and David Thompson, are worthy to be remembered with the same honour as Alexander Mackenzie.

Between 6 August, 1804, and 27 April, 1808, Mackenzie

represented Huntingdon county in the legislature of Lower Canada. It is apparent, however, that he had no interest in a political career.

He was now ready to retire from active involvement in the trade and in November, 1805, as he departed for England, he wrote to Roderick, 'Never mind the folly of the times for my own part I am determined to make myself as comfortable as circumstances will allow. I have a large field before me—I do not leave Canada without regret.'

His chosen field during the next few years, during which he lived chiefly in London and seldom crossed the Atlantic, was to work for the establishment on the Pacific Coast of a British company organized along the lines he had already advocated. In 1808 he made a formal proposal but nothing came of it. In 1810 he went to Montreal, probably to organize a renewed request by the North West Company itself. This was formally put to the British government in 1811. By now the whole issue was urgent in the extreme. Lewis and Clark, sent by President Jefferson, had reached the mouth of the Columbia as long ago as November, 1805, and John Jacob Astor had just founded Astoria, a trading post at the mouth of the river. There was real and visible danger that Britain would soon find her overland access to the Pacific denied by the advance of American claims. But nothing was done.

As we look at the map of North America, we see how vital it is for Canada to have an opening on the Pacific. We see also how valuable is the possession of a great river which provides, in the midst of a wilderness of mountains, a continuous valley along which railways and roads can run, which offers some alluvial land suitable for farming, and which terminates in a delta or estuary giving shelter to shipping. One such river Canada possesses—the Fraser. It would be beneficial indeed to her trade and transport if she also possessed, within her own territory, the lower valley and mouth of the Columbia. Canadians find it difficult to understand why Britain allowed this territory, to which a British claim could so easily have been established, to slip away and they tend to lump together this business and the later settlement of the boundary with Alaska which has left Canada without an opening on the Pacific north of Portland Canal.

It is only fair, however, to put oneself in the position of the British government at this time. Napoleon was at the height of his power; only Russia and Britain were beyond his continental grasp and against Britain he was bent on enforcing a blockade to exclude her goods from Europe and ruin her commerce. In 1812 he invaded Russia and seemed on the point of dominating Europe from the North Sea to the Ural mountains. At the same time war broke out between Britain and America and three American expeditions set out to invade Canada. In the midst of such events, the British government may be forgiven for neglecting the long-term prospects of British trade and colonization in a region so remote and unexplored as New Caledonia, as Simon Fraser named the territory he found on the other side of the Rockies, which he thought, from what his mother had told him, must resemble Scotland. Fraser, twelve years younger than Mackenzie, did not enter the service of the North West Company till 1792 but he was in a very real sense Mackenzie's successor, in that he extended the Company's operations into what is now northern British Columbia and accomplished the supremely hazardous exploration of the lower reaches of the Fraser River.

If the British government was blind to its strategic interests and the possibilities of trade in the far west, Mackenzie and his partners, it must be conceded, were equally oblivious of a matter quite as vital to the future of Canada—its settlement by colonists, who would cultivate the land and form stable communities. For anyone who admires Mackenzie, to tell how he obstructed settlement in the west is an unhappy task. In his struggle with Lord Selkirk, his limitations are all too clearly revealed.

As Mackenzie's connection with Peter Pond throws a great deal of light on his early career, so his relation with Selkirk illuminates the years after his retirement.

Thomas Douglas, born in June, 1771, in Kirkcudbright-shire, the seventh son of a noble family, had, by the untimely death of his brother, inherited an earldom and become Lord Selkirk at the age of twenty-eight. He was a natural philan-thropist and deeply concerned about the cotters and crofters who were being pushed out of the Highlands. In 1803 he led a group of them to Prince Edward Island, to establish new homes. Later he turned his attention to the fertile prairie land of the Red River and in 1808 he was buying stock in the Hudson's Bay Company, on joint account with Alexander Mackenzie. Shares had fallen to three-fifths of their par value, because of competition from the North-Westers and a renewal of the conflict with Napoleon. Selkirk advanced money to Mackenzie, who was short of liquid capital. By 1810, how-ever, their association came to an end.

Early in 1811, Selkirk made a formal proposal to the Hudson's Bay Company, by which he was to receive an immense grant of land on the Canadian prairies, in return for which he would establish a colony of farmers in the Red River area and supply the Company with two hundred men per annum. His optimism absorbed all difficulties, even the six hundred miles of wilderness between Hudson Bay and the most suitable farm land in the Red River valley, even the climate, with its frequent sub-zero winter temperatures. The

Hudson's Bay Company's committee accepted the proposal, whereupon Mackenzie, whose interest gave him a voice in the Company's proceedings, insisted that it be brought to a general meeting of stockholders.

On both sides of the Atlantic the North-Westers rallied their forces in opposition. In May, Simon McGillivray wrote to his brother William, in Montreal, 'His Lordship is a designing and dangerous character—and Sir Alexander has not been sufficiently aware of him.' This may be unfair to Mackenzie who, a year or more earlier, had warned his associates concerning Selkirk, 'He will put the North West Company to a greater expense than you seem to apprehend, and, had the Company sacrificed £20,000, which might have secured a preponderance in the stock of the Hudson's Bay Company, it would have been money well spent.'

When the General Court of the Hudson's Bay Company met at the end of May, 1811, the grant to Lord Selkirk was confirmed by more than two-thirds of the votes of the shareholders. The North-Westers had failed in their attempt to block the dispatch of a party of colonists to the Red River; their arguments and protests had been in vain. But there was to be no end to their efforts to ruin the enterprise.

There is unfortunately no question about Mackenzie's animus against Selkirk and the colony. Before the expedition started, he was visited by the leader of the party, Miles Macdonnell. He seized this occasion to assert that the North West Company would not tolerate the colony and could incite the Indians against it.

The initial sufferings of the Red River colonists were appalling. Nothing in their experience had prepared them for the endless winter months, the lethal temperatures, the sense of isolation combined with a desperate shortage of food. Among the successive attempts to reinforce them, the most significant was probably the dispatch in 1813 of a party numbering more than ninety, chiefly drawn from Kildonan, in the extreme north of Scotland. They settled on both banks of the Red River and took firm root as a community, calling their new home Kildonan. Here was established, a generation later, in 1851, the first Presbyterian church in western Canada.

Between the new colony and the North West Company relations went from bad to worse. Macdonnell was dangerously short of food and took a calculated risk in order to keep supplies under his own control. He was legally Governor of the grant held by Selkirk and in this capacity issued a proclamation forbidding the export of food, except under licence, from the territory. This was a direct affront to the North-Westers and to the métis associated with the trade. (The latter were of mixed European and Indian blood, métis being a French word derived from the Latin *miscere*, to mix.) A compromise was reached, after the threat of a pitched battle, but the resulting peace was extremely precarious.

In 1815, by a mixture of fraud and force, most of the settlers were dispossessed of their homes and some thirty buildings burned. But three men saved the blacksmith's shop, with some stores, defending it by force of arms. Many of the evicted settlers came back, and life went on.

On 19 June, 1816, a parley between some sixty métis, and about a third of that number of troops and settlers, turned into a battle in which the métis overran their opponents and gave no quarter to the wounded. Known as the Seven Oaks Massacre, it resulted in the death of Robert Semple, the governor of the settlement, and about twenty others. The colonists were forced to leave under threat of death.

Selkirk was already on his way to Red River, with a troop

of disbanded soldiers. He took possession of the North-Westers' headquarters at Fort William and detained a number of the Company's leaders. They were sent back to Canada to stand trial. The North West Company in turn brought action against Selkirk. Although he was able to restore the colony, he was less successful in the courts and was ordered to pay damages of £2,000. He returned to England at the end of 1818. Suffering from a tubercular condition, he had less than eighteen months of life before him. He died at Pau, within sight of the Pyrenees, on 8 April, 1820, dictating, during his last days, his plans for an experimental farm at Red River.

On 26 March, 1821, the North West Company and the Hudson's Bay Company were amalgamated.

The opposition between fur trader and settler is one variant of a conflict as old as Cain and Abel. He whose livelihood comes from animals—whether wild or domesticated—on an open range of country will fear him who erects fences, claims legal possession of lands and makes regulations governing transport. The settlers establishing their farms will in turn fear the shifting opportunism, the arrogance and the armed force of the fur hunters. The fur trade, a fiercely extractive and of necessity ever widening operation, demanded freedom of action for its agents, a freedom intolerable to the farmer whose dependence on the seasons called for foresight, prudence and control of resources.

How much Mackenzie had to do with the struggle for power on the banks of the Red River it is impossible to say. One would like to believe that, when he married, in 1812, and retired to an estate on Moray Firth, his antagonisms faded. But this is by no means probable. When Selkirk put his case against the North West partners in *A Sketch of the British Fur Trade in North America*, published in London in

1816, a reply appeared the next year entitled *A Narrative of Occurrences in the Indian Countries of North America*. The preface to this reply by the North-Westers brings in Mackenzie's name: 'Sir Alexander Mackenzie, to whose authority Lord Selkirk so often appeals and whom he so often misrepresents, was desirous of taking up the discussion, an intention the execution of which circumstances alone have hitherto delayed.' These circumstances must have included the state of his health at this time.

What we know of his marriage throws little if any light upon his inner life or private personality. It appears that, following 'the custom of the country', he took an Indian squaw to live with him in the west. Their son Andrew was in the service of the North West Company and was baptized in Montreal. No one appears to know what happened to the Indian girl. 'La façon du pays' had very varied consequences. Some of the traders, when they left the country, left the squaw and their children to another man. Alexander Ross, the fur trader and historian, married, about 1813, the daughter of an Okanagan Indian chief. About 1825 he retired from the Oregon fur trade and moved to Red River where he settled and gave his children a first-class education. He was sheriff of Assiniboia from 1839 to 1852 and his descendants played prominent parts in the government and development of the community. Mackenzie, as we have seen, had other ambitions.

His marriage, in 1812, to Geddes Mackenzie was by all accounts a very happy one. She was renowned for her beauty and was of the same clan as her husband though not directly related. It is possible that he met her in London; he had been living near Tower Hill where her father's London house was situated. Soon after their marriage they moved to Scotland, to an estate called Avoch, on Moray Firth. This had once belonged to her father but at his death passed into the hands of trustees, from whom her husband now purchased it.

He was now a country gentleman and, at the age of forty-eight, had fulfilled his ambition to retire on the proceeds of his fur trading. He was well off, well situated with his Scottish estate and a London house on Jermyn Street, and well thought of in society. His friendship with the Duke of Kent is evidenced in a letter he received from Kensington Palace in November, 1819. It begins, 'My dear Sir Alexander,—I have gratefully to acknowledge your favour of the 26th ulto. received on the 30th, covering the copy of your letter to our mutual worthy friend Mr Charles Forbes, for which fresh mark of your friendship and attachment I beg to express my warmest thanks.' Further on, we get an unexpected glimpse of Queen Victoria at a very tender age: 'I ran over in the course of last week to Devonshire to look out for a house that might suit the Duchess to pass the next four months in, near the Sea, to enjoy the benefit of the mild air of that part of our Coast and of the tepid sea Baths, and I trust we shall be able to manage our remove thither in the course of this month. In the meanwhile I know it will give you pleasure to learn that she is getting over the effects of weaning her Infant, as well as I could possibly expect, and that our little child does not appear to thrive the less for the change. Sincerely hoping that Lady McKenzie will get over her accouchement with every possible comfort, and with every sentiment of the warmest friendship and regard for yourself.—I remain ever, My dear Sir Alexander, Yours most faithfully, Edward.'

Mackenzie could not have guessed that this Infant would become the object of loyalty and focus of imperial sentiment in the whole area he had penetrated as a wilderness, and this over a period lasting until the beginning of the present century. It would have pleased him, had he known.

In January, 1819, he sat down and wrote a long letter to the faithful Roderick, who was now married, with young children, and still in the North West Company. He himself had two children, Margaret Geddes, born in 1816, and Alexander, two years younger. Before the year was out, his third child, George, would be born. The letter is probably the last he wrote to his cousin and he may have sensed this; it is very much a summing up. His agreement with the Company will soon expire and he is no longer in direct touch with much that goes on across the Atlantic. 'Occurrences with Lord Selkirk and the HB Company are so various and numerous that it would require a volume to detail and comment upon them. Most of the prominent events I learn from the public prints. Upon the whole they have not turned out so disastrous to the NW Company as might naturally have been apprehended. The losses sustained in the country though severe and serious have been in a considerable degree recompensed by the high prices obtained for the furs, the sales of which were certainly managed with great judgment in London.'

He had reason to be interested in the financial success of the North-Westers, though he was no longer active. 'They will have a large amount to account to me, the present agents do not seem disposed to reduce it as they have not paid me a shilling of principal or interest since I became a partner under the firm of Sir Alexander Mackenzie & Co. . . . I trust Mrs Mackenzie and your young family are continuing in their usual good health. Margaret must now be a stout lady; My namesake about finishing his education for college; had you sent him to this country it might have been as well. [The boy did well in any case, became Lieutenant-Colonel

Alexander Mackenzie and lived until 1862.] What do you think of sending Roderick Charles here when he is fit, we have two good academies in this country, at Thain and Fortrose. I shall have a little fellow, if God spare him, this day eleven months old that would accompany him. Our little girl is very thriving. Her mother has not recovered her usual health since her last confinement and I have at last been overtaken with the consequences of my sufferings in the North West.'

It is not clear what Mackenzie was suffering from though it is thought to have been Bright's disease, a progressively degenerative condition of the kidneys. Neither is it clear how, except by the general strain upon his constitution, the hardships of his travels conduced to this condition. But Mackenzie himself clearly thought so. He was never the same man after the intense and continuous effort of the great journeys. He continues, 'The symptoms of the disorder are very disagreeable and most uncomfortable. The exercise of walking, particularly uphill, brings on a headache, stupor or dead pain which at once pervades the whole frame, attended with listlessness and apathy which I cannot well describe. Exercise in a carriage, if not violent, has a beneficial effect. The great doctor Hamilton of Edinburg calls it a shake of the constitution and I am acting now under his guidance. The only medicine he has prescribed is pills of his own which I take every evening.

'By a letter from Angus Bethune, I heard of Donald's situation on the Columbia. [This brother of Roderick's had a long fur trading career, with the North-Westers, with Astor and with the Hudson's Bay Company and became Governor of Red River.] It is one of considerable personal risk, but advantageous, had he been able to reach the proper hunting-grounds.

'It is now believed there are plenty beaver in that country, and it will be very hard if it is wrested from us through the ignorance of our negotiators. That crafty, cunning statesman Gallatin (Astor's friend) was the principal negotiator on the part of the americans. He would be too many for our people who are governed more by theory than practice. . . .'

The tactics of Gallatin, pursued in these negotiations, which resulted in the Convention of 1818, and in further negotiations begun in 1826, were ultimately successful. After deadlocks and joint occupations, the Oregon territory south of the 49th parallel passed to the United States in 1846. Mackenzie's fears were only too well founded.

His letter concludes: 'Lady Mackenzie is sitting by me, and the children are playing on the floor. The former joins me most cordially in kind regards to you Mrs Mackenzie and your young family.—Yours very truly and sincerely.'

Taken as a whole, this letter has the air of a farewell message and such it proved to be. He had a little more than a year to live. A letter from Kenneth Dowie, Alexander's nephew, addressed to Roderick says simply, 'It is with the deepest regret I have to inform you of the death of my uncle, Sir Alexander Mackenzie. Accompanied by Lady Mackenzie and children, he was on his way from Edinburgh to Ross-shire, and was suddenly taken ill at Mulnain [Mulinearn], near Dunkeld, on the 11th March, and expired the following morning.' He was buried in the old churchyard at Avoch.

Between Mackenzie's death among his own mountains, near the Pass of Killicrankie, and Selkirk's death in the shadow of the Pyrenees, scarcely a month intervened.

In 1830 Geddes Mackenzie was paid £10,000 by the Hudson's Bay Company in settlement of the claims her husband's estate had upon them through his interest in the North West Company, which they had absorbed in 1821.

She continued to live at Avoch and in London, where she had a house in Clarges Street. The children were well educated. Margaret, whose painting in water-colour won her a reputation, died in 1888; Alexander, who succeeded to the estate upon his mother's death in 1860, lived until 1894; George, who became a wine merchant, died in 1880. Of the three children, only Alexander married; his family consisted of three sons and two daughters. The family lost most of their father's books and manuscripts in a fire which destroyed the house at Avoch in 1832.

VI

Achievement in Retrospect

The Fortunes of the Fur Trade

After Mackenzie's departure from Athabasca, the North-Westers established a web of canoe routes, pinned down by forts, both up toward the Arctic and into what are now British Columbia and the State of Washington. Notable, in this programme of expansion, was Simon Fraser's courageous descent, in 1808, through the boiling current between canyon walls, to the lower reaches of the river named for him. Notable too was David Thompson's survey of the whole length of the Columbia, in 1811. At the mouth, he found the newly established Fort Astoria, which, three years later, the North-Westers bought and renamed Fort George.

On the other side of the ledger commitments were being made which would wipe out these gains. The basic difficulty was the inability of the Company to establish a genuine Pacific trade. No commercial exchange could be built up on the casual visits of predatory captains, bent on exterminating the sea-otter. American ships and traders from overland had no reason to link up with Canadian enterprise; from 1812 to 1814, the two countries were, in fact, at war. The North-Westers could not trade direct with China, because of the East India Company's monopoly.

Mackenzie remained keenly interested in Arctic exploration. There is a fortunate record of his meeting Sir John

Franklin, who was preparing to sail for the far North. 'A short time before I left London I had the pleasure and advantage of an interview with the late Sir Alexander Mackenzie, who was one of the two persons who had visited the coast we were to explore. He afforded me, in the most open and kind manner, much valuable information and advice.' The meeting probably took place in 1818.

Nothing, however, came of British efforts to pierce the ice and find a north-west passage. The Pacific remained immensely remote and, in the end, Mackenzie's hopes of a whaling and fur-trading combine, backed by the British government, fell to the ground.

The result was an impossible fanning out process, by which goods from Montreal had to be lifted to the remote north and west, the proceeds in furs being painfully returned by the same routes. Colin Robertson, an employee of the North West Company who went over to the Hudson's Bay Company, wrote in 1812, 'It is not many years since the Canadian establishments of the Fur Traders in North America extended no further than the banks of Lake Superior; but now their boundaries are the Atlantic, the Pacific and Frozen Oceans; however I am afraid their ambition and enterprise have carried them too far, as these distant settlements oblige them to employ three sets of men to bring the returns of McKenzie's River and New Caledonia [Fraser's name for the Pacific region he had visited] to Montreal.'

What drove the North-Westers to these extreme exertions, on an over-extended, fanned out network of routes, was fierce competition for a limited resource. A letter written in 1812 'to Messrs. McTavish, Fraser & Company, Inglis, Ellice & Company, Sir Alexander Mackenzie' speaks of the difficulty of competing with American traders in the Columbia River area, 'our only remaining Beaver country'. There is a great scarcity of beaver, it adds, throughout the whole north-west region east of the Rockies. 'This has been so much felt for the last two years that the country in its present state cannot support our establishments of partners, clerks and canoe-men, so that there is a necessity for extending the field, were there no intruders in the country to menace us.'

More serious than American rivalry was the old competi-tion between North-Westers and Hudson's Bay men. Looking at it dispassionately, as one belonging to neither party, Franklin commented, 'This mode of carrying on the trade not only causes the amount of furs, collected by either of the two Companies, to depend more on the activity of their agents, the knowledge they possess of the motions of the Indians, and the quantity of rum they carry, than upon the liberality of the credits they give, but is also productive of an increasing deterioration of the character of the Indians and will probably ultimately prove destructive to the fur trade itself. Indeed the evil has already in part recoiled upon the traders; for the Indians long deceived have become deceivers in their turn and not unfrequently after having incurred a heavy debt at one post, move off to another, to play the same game. In some cases the rival posts have entered into a mutual agreement, to trade only with the Indians they have respectively fitted out; but such treaties being seldom adhered to, prove a fertile subject for disputes and the differences have more than once been decided by force of arms. To carry on the contest, the two Companies are obliged to employ a great many servants, whom they maintain often with much difficulty, and always at a con-siderable expense.'

The minutes of the North West Company, for the early 1800's, record various attempts to cut down expenses. It is not without some amusement that we see the lords of the lakes and forest urged to practise a little economy. A Proprietor taking a train of canoes into the western wintering grounds shall stay with them, not dash about in a light canoe. He shall not take baggage in excess of 720 pounds and shall not have more than one man personally attending him. A second attendant will cost him a fine of £50. In the spring, one light canoe, starting from Athabasca, will collect written reports of Proprietors for delivery at headquarters. They may not, when they themselves come down, bring more than two buffalo robes, or two dressed skins, as their own property. The voyageurs are absolutely forbidden to bring in furs in their own account, for private profit.

The number of women and children maintained by the Company was also a matter of concern. It was therefore resolved that 'no man whatsoever, either partner, Clerk, or Engagé, belonging to the Concern shall henceforth take or suffer to be taken under any pretence, whatsoever, any woman or maid from any of the tribes of Indians now known or who may hereafter become known in this Country to live with him after the fashion of the North West, that is to say, to live with him within the Company Houses or Fort and be maintained at the expence of the Concern'.

Mackenzie himself, in order to cut down the costs of transport, had, long ago, as early as 1794, suggested that the Company try to get an outlet through Hudson Bay. A glance at the map will show the advantages of this route, providing that ships can bring in a cargo as well as take one out and that trade moves in an annual cycle, requirements fulfilled by the nature of the fur trade. It is quite likely that his acquisition of Hudson's Bay Company stock, after his return to England was with this end in view. He did not easily relinquish any project he had in mind.

Although the North-Westers were willing, in 1805, to offer

their rivals £2,000 per annum for access to the route through the Bay and, when that came to nothing, proposed in 1810 to fix a boundary line between the two operations which would have meant the loss of seventeen of their own posts, in the end all these attempts at peaceful settlement failed. Animosity reached its climax over Lord Selkirk's settlement in the Red River Valley.

The Fur Trade and Canada's Boundaries

The Treaty of Paris, in 1783, which recognized the independence of the thirteen American colonies, also indicated the boundary between the United States and what is now Canada. The line passed through the Great Lakes, on to Lake of the Woods, from the north-west corner of which it was to go 'on a due west course to the River Mississippi'. It was discovered, however, that the river lay entirely south of such a line and a new agreement, in 1818, laid down the 49th parallel of latitude as the boundary up to the Rocky Mountains. It is from this point on that Mackenzie's voyages affect the issue.

His own conception of British claims is given in an appendix to the *Voyages*—the line from Lake of the Woods 'is also said to run West to the Mississippi, which it may do, by giving it a good deal of Southing, but not otherwise; as the source of that river does not extend further North than latitude 47·38. North, where it is no more than a small brook; consequently, if Great Britain retains the right of entering it along the line of division, it must be in a lower latitude, and wherever that may be, the line must be continued West, till it terminates in the Pacific Ocean, to the South of the Columbia. This division [of fur trading territory] is then bounded by the Pacific Ocean on the West, the Frozen Sea and Hudson's Bay on the North and East. The Russians, indeed may claim with justice, the islands and coast from Behring's Straits to Cook's Entry.'

It is worth our while to run a finger along this line and try to reconstruct Mackenzie's thinking as well as the reasons for Canada's not having achieved these limits.

The provision in the Treaty of Paris for a line which cut the Mississippi was to ensure British access to it, as navigable water. A further provision allowed free navigation of the river by both British and Americans. To fur traders this would have been an invaluable asset; it would have given access to the Gulf of Mexico. It was inevitable, however, that Americans would think of the agreement as providing for a line running west from Lake of the Woods and be quite unmoved by its denying to the British all rights on the Mississippi. The compromise of 1818, like the settlement of every other dispute over Canada's boundaries in the west, strongly favoured American claims.

Our next point of attention is the Columbia Valley. It will be recalled that the mouth of the Columbia was one of the points where Mackenzie urged the British government to establish a military and naval presence. He was urgently aware that it was part of a no-man's-land into which any one of several powers might quickly move.

An interesting possibility appears when we try to forecast what would have occurred if Mackenzie's recommendations had been listened to and implemented, if the three Pacific posts he envisaged had all been established. One can easily come to the conclusion that the territory which became the American states of Washington and Oregon would now be part of Canada. To the present writer, who lives in British Columbia and has worked as a farm hand in Oregon, this thought has a nostalgic glow about it, the romantic attractiveness of a surrendered inheritance. To Canadians in general it has the air of a real possibility unluckily lost and it adds to Mackenzie's figure the stature of a prophet unheeded. This, however, is not the whole story.

The Columbia was probably discovered by Spaniards coming by sea from Mexico. On old charts there is a 'Rio de San Roque' in approximately the right latitude. In 1792, a Captain Gray, from Boston, explored the mouth of the river and gave it the name of his trading vessel, the *Columbia*. In 1807 David Thompson crossed the Rockies and built Kootenae House, the first trading post on the river. In 1811 he surveyed accurately the whole course of the river, from Fort Astoria, which had just been established by John Jacob Astor's men, to its source, a distance of over a thousand miles.

Astor's company lost three ships in a row and was then, in 1812, faced with the hazards of war which broke out between Britain and the United States. It adroitly sold out for $80,500 to the North West Company, which changed the name of the post to Fort George. Fort George passed to the Hudson's Bay Company in the merger of 1821. In 1818, however, a treaty between Britain and America had provided for joint occupation of the territory. The expedition of Lewis and Clark, sent by President Jefferson, reached the lower valley of the Columbia in 1805 and from 1838 onward there was a flow of American settlers. In 1843 these demanded union with the United States. This suited the Democratic party, which was eager to use as a campaign platform the prospect of annexing Texas and Oregon, a programme likely to appeal to Americans of both North and South. They won the election in 1844 and in 1845 Texas was taken over and war declared against Mexico, at the conclusion of which New Mexico and California were ceded to the United States. Had President Polk gone on to press the claim expressed in his party's pre-election slogan, 'Fifty-four forty, or fight', he would have been obliged to fight because this is the latitude of the southern tip of the Alaskan 'panhandle'. The American demand was intolerable; it would have meant the loss of our entire Pacific coast and have shut Canada off from any access to the sea. Earl Cathcart, governor of Canada and commander of the forces, made extensive preparations for defence. Britain's strongest weapon, of course, would have been a blockade of American ports. A compromise settlement, however, was reached by the terms of which the territory was divided at the 49th parallel and the Strait of Juan de Fuca.

Let us suppose, however, for the sake of argument, that Mackenzie's advice to the British government in 1802 had in fact been followed and that a post at the mouth of the Columbia had been set up before Astor had thought of doing so. It seems certain that, even so, the main concern of the British interests involved would have been the fur trade. This trade would have been certain to dwindle away and give place to farming, lumbering and mining; a great influx of American citizens would in any case have occurred. If, in these circumstances, Britain had indeed possessed a legal claim on what is now Washington and Oregon, the population would nevertheless have been chiefly American and it is not difficult to conclude that, when the Mexican war had succeeded, Polk or some later president would have gone to war with Britain, in default of a compromise settlement. The stakes were high and America has acquired Louisiana, Texas, New Mexico and California with little difficulty. Later on, over territory of far less importance to the U.S.A., during the Alaska boundary dispute of 1903, Roosevelt did threaten to use force and Canadian claims were largely surrendered, the northern half of British Columbia being to this day deprived of any westward access to the ocean.

The point of this recital is that there are good grounds for believing that Mackenzie's great journeys achieved their complete potential, though this was less than he had hoped for. We must admire the imagination which directed twenty-three pioneer families, in the spring of 1841, to move from Red River to the lower Columbia and the fortitude that sustained the long journey, their horses and cattle accompanying. But a second attempt to bring in British colonists did not succeed, whereas, after the Lewis and Clark expedition, American settlers came in numbers over the Oregon trail. What Mackenzie did help to ensure, by his journeys, by the publication of the *Voyages*, by representations to government and by an appeal to public opinion, was the existence of British Columbia as a colony and, in due course, a Canadian province.

There remains the boundary with Alaska to consider. It is possible that the British government's disregard of Mackenzie's recommendation to establish a post at 55° North latitude was crucial. Had trade been established in harbours up the coast from such a centre, Canada's total loss of access to the sea above 55° might perhaps have been prevented. In view of the American threat of force, in the joint commission of 1903, which settled the matter, it is difficult to say.

The border between Alaska and the Yukon is ignored in most discussions of Canada's boundaries. It runs for seven hundred miles through wild, potentially rich, but almost uninhabited territory. The fur traders who followed Mackenzie up the valley of his river established a claim to the country which, reinforced by gold miners who arrived in the 90's, led to the present line being drawn. Once again Mackenzie's voyage served, in the long run, the Canadian national interest.

As a pendant to this account of Mackenzie and our western boundaries, an odd story of Napoleonic ambitions is worth recalling.

One of the few things saved from the Avoch fire is a French translation of Mackenzie's *Voyages*, in three volumes, stamped with the French eagle, which was actually in Napoleon's possession on St Helena. The story of the French translation was told to a relative of Mackenzie's when on a visit to Stockholm in 1824. The narrator was none other than the king of Sweden, Napoleon's old marshal, Bernadotte.

His story was that, about 1812, Napoleon hoped to make an agreement with the United States which would allow him to use New Orleans as a base for an attack on British North America. A French expedition was to move up the Mississippi and take Canada by surprise from the rear.

There is documentary evidence that this was indeed Napoleon's intention and not a figment of the old marshal's imagination. He was to organize and take command of the expedition and, as the *Voyages* was known to be a unique and recent source of information about the waterways of the west, the 'huge quarto' was procured through smugglers and rendered into French for Bernadotte's use.

He told Mackenzie's relative that he had read and re-read the *Voyages*, with great admiration, and he added, laughing, that he could then almost picture himself attacking Canada down the canoe routes from the west. But, instead, the Russian campaign had been launched, with all its disastrous consequences. A strange story for a king of Sweden to be telling.

If the Canadian campaign was planned for 1812, it was not as mad an idea as we might think. American anger against Britain led to actual war in that year and Napoleon may have supposed that he could combine his naval forces with those of America to ensure the passage of an army to New Orleans and that the American government would furnish supplies. If he intended simply to move an army up the valleys of the Mississippi and the Ohio so as to reach the Great Lakes region, Mackenzie's *Voyages* would not have been particularly relevant. That Bernadotte was asked to study this work, smuggled across the Channel and translated for his special use, indicates that Napoleon had designs on the far west as well. It is an interesting speculation: suppose France had occupied upper and lower Canada and taken control of the far north and west, what then would have been the American response? When faced with a French military presence in Maximilian's Mexico, a generation later, the American government forced its withdrawal in 1867. A withdrawal of British troops from Canada was planned for 1870 and only delayed a few months by the Riel rebellion. American anxiety to see the continent cleared of European troops was very visible.

It therefore seems probable that, had the French taken possession of Canada from Pacific to Atlantic, their troops would ultimately have withdrawn under American pressure, soon after 1815. It is a nice speculation what would then have happened to Canadian sovereignty.

The Legend of Mackenzie's Voyages

Two hundred years have passed since Mackenzie first walked the streets of Stornoway and he is turning into a legend. It seems likely that the process will continue and it is tempting to consider what elements in the record lend themselves to this kind of change.

In a longer vista of time than we at present command, Canadians will probably see the voyages to Arctic and Pacific as the Greeks saw the fabulous voyage of Argonauts to fetch the fleece. The story of building a ship and navigating it between clashing Symplegades, in search of a golden reward, was expanded, as Greece in later centuries became more and more concerned with exploration and the founding of new cities. Beyond this, Mackenzie's myth does not extend itself. The rivalry with McTavish, the disagreement with Selkirk, the vain efforts to interest British ministers: these are anti-climactic elements adding nothing to the simple achievement.

He will also be seen in the company of his peers. They include Henry Kelsey who, in 1691, travelled far enough westward to encounter buffalo on the prairies; Pierre de la Vérendrye and his sons, of whom two, in 1743, reached the foothills of the American Rockies; Anthony Henday, the first white man to see the Canadian Rockies, which he could discern in the west as he was seeking furs in the area that now lies between Edmonton and Calgary; Peter Fidler, who between 1792 and 1795 devotedly explored the South Saskatchewan and Athabasca Rivers; and Samuel Hearne, who in the face of great hardship, made the return journey from Hudson Bay to the Arctic in 1770–2. On the Pacific side we must add Russian, Spanish and English navigators who made their landfalls on the west coast: Vitus Bering in 1771, Juan Perez in 1774, Cook in 1778 and Vancouver in 1792–4. The expeditions of Thompson and Fraser along the great rivers have already been mentioned.

This tradition was carried on by such men as James and Joseph Tyrrell, who in 1893 made a famous journey across the Barren Lands, the great subarctic area stretching from Great Slave and Great Bear Lakes to Hudson Bay, where the ground is permanently frozen to within a few inches of the surface. The best known representative of the tradition in our own times is Vilhjalmar Stefansson.

The eighteenth-century explorers in whose company Mac-kenzie belongs stand somewhat separate, in one's imagina-tion, from three other groups—explorers of the American west, who had no reason to move north into what is now Canada, but reached toward Californian and Oregon terri-tory; the navigators who, from the Atlantic side, pushed their vessels into the ice in a vain, heroic search for a north-west passage; and the great French explorers of a much earlier era, who for enterprise and élan have never been surpassed: Champlain, who reached the Georgian Bay of Lake Huron in 1615; Louis Jolliet and Father Jacques Marquette, whose canoe was on the Mississippi in 1673; and the great La Salle, to whom fell the honour of following the river to the Gulf of Mexico, in 1682.

Mackenzie and his contemporaries share the legendary quality of a period marked by a great capacity for physical exertion, combined with rational planning and a matter-of-fact emotional approach. The legend takes charge as Carlyle writes of Frederick the Great in the Seven Years' War. The single indomitable will drives bodies of troops along moun-tain defiles and over rivers, through storms of musketry and cannonading, with fearful losses, to their goal. The survivors regroup, reinforcements appear and the next strategic objec-tive is announced. With equal relentlessness, Frederick drives his own body. The same pattern can be sensed in accounts, true or fictional, of the British navy, from Anson's matter-of-fact achievement of an impossible circumnavigation of the world to the convincing exploits of Captain Hornblower.

It seems probable that this attitude of mind and this readi-ness of the body to perform what the mind dictates have something to do with Descartes's view of the world. God, he believed, had created two classes of substance which com-prise total reality: thinking minds and extended bodies. It is certain that a vague but powerful Cartesianism affected the actions of military strategists: the private soldier was a mechanism ordered by a superior intelligence. In the early states of the Industrial Revolution the factory 'operative', as his name implied, fitted into the total mechanism, similarly ordered from above.

Technical progress of various kinds had much the same effect. We are accustomed to think of mechanisms for the development of power as a means of liberating human beings from physical toil. The exact opposite may at first occur. As soon as superior artillery tactics make possible a continuous hail of shot down a given avenue, armies discipline themselves to march across the line of fire. When improved methods of navigation make possible immense voyages and the accurate plotting of courses, on both counts the officers and crew find themselves bound by an exacting discipline which demands that their bodies respond with unflagging precision.

Among eighteenth-century explorers not concerned with North America, Mungo Park comes to mind as the perfect example of a complete disregard of personal convenience, comfort and safety, in the pursuit of a set objective. His second journey, in which he followed the course of the Niger, revealed powers of persistence and endurance which became an end in themselves, so that his death seems incidental to his triumph.

Heroic persistence is, of course, common in the human record. What marks this set of eighteenth-century men is that their objectives are ostensibly mundane, in contrast to the religious zeal of Jesuit or Moravian travellers into the unknown; that the commitment of their powers to the task is so complete as to seem automatic; and, finally, that their tangible personal gain seems quite incommensurate with their achievement. Mackenzie's financial success was considerable but he could have made as much or more out of the trade if he had let others go exploring. The journal shows a man totally absorbed in carrying out, for its own sake, what he had begun.

The legend of Alexander Mackenzie is already assuming a shape different from that of the traditional historical record. The fur trade falls into the background; the explorer's habits of thought and traits of character emerge more clearly. He shows the classic powers of analysis and synthesis to a far great degree than his associates.

In a letter from Fort Forks, dated 9 May 1793, and addressed to Roderick, he says, 'I send you a couple of guineas; the rest I take with me to traffic with the Russians.' It seems likely, then, that even at this point he was hoping that Peter Pond's map was not completely misleading and that a great waterway did indeed run due west. He was at that moment at about 56° North latitude and if he had been able to move approximately along that parallel he would have come to salt water within the compass of the Russian coastal trade. He may have had in mind the trading post, clearly Russian, which the Dog Rib and Hare Indians had told him about on his first voyage. It was, they said, at the mouth of the great river of the west. They were most likely referring to the Yukon River which, in actual fact, reaches the sea on the remote far side of Alaska twenty-five hundred miles from where Mackenzie was penning his message to Roderick.

On the strength of these guineas in his pocket, we can see him, as his journey progressed, probing in his mind no less than six alternate routes to the Pacific: the Mackenzie, a river of disappointment as he termed it; the Yukon, which he had heard of and still hoped he might reach; the non-existent river of Pond's map, flowing into Cook's inlet; his actual overland route to Bella Coola; the Fraser, into whose canyon he rightly hesitated to plunge; and the Columbia, which, like the Yukon, he had vaguely heard of but had no means of locating or reaching. On this view, his analysis seems truly admirable. In a jumble of mountains which he had not known existed (Pond's map showed a single range of Rockies), his reserve of bullets lost and his canoe shattered, his logistics were as nearly faultless as we could ask. With limited, inaccurate and shifting data, he made a continually changing analysis of the situation and arrived at the best decision possible in the circumstances, one which brought him to his goal.

His desire for synthesis, when his objectives were obtained, is equally clear and needs no further proof. Taking positive views, he tried to unite British territorial interests, to organize commerce under the aegis of the Crown, to consolidate and stabilize the fur trade. The lamentable exception of his relation with Selkirk can only be admitted and deplored.

An alternating pattern, of failure and success, appears in Mackenzie's life and the subsequent story of the things he cared about. He came to Athabasca as the result of a merging of interests to put an end to a murderous struggle; his disappointment over the Arctic journey spurred him to make the westward trial; his defeat by McTavish was succeeded, after the latter's death, by another junction of competitors; his own death and Selkirk's was followed by the North-Westers' joining the Hudson's Bay Company; though the Americans uniformly got the advantage in disputes over western boundaries, Canada has held a territory in which a viable community could become a great nation. It remains to hope for a continuation of this pattern, past the crisis of French-Canadian separatism into a future of assured and amicable unity between the two cultures.

The most natural and perhaps most enduring element in the legend growing about Alexander Mackenzie is his association with landscape. He is already the *genius loci* of many wild places in the West.

Some forty miles downstream from Alexandria, a bad road leaves the Fraser valley and twists for three hundred miles across the tableland known as the Fraser Plateau, traversing a rugged, lightly forested, largely unexploited country so thinly inhabited that one can drive past a named settlement without being aware of it. South-west, as the route rises and talls, the great icefields of the Coast Range glitter inter- mittently. The western edge of the plateau reveals itself as the road plunges for twelve miles to reach sea level. It becomes a mere shelf, hacked out by the combined efforts of people from the cattle ranches above and those from the Bella Coola valley down below. With their own bulldozers, dynamite and picks and shovels they have clawed out a corniche, so steep in places that the driver of an ascending car may find his view of the road blocked by his own radia- tor. Without guards or signs, it narrows in places to a crumbling lip above a drop it is best to refrain from measur- ing with the eye. At the beginning of the descent, we are in a region of small pines and scanty rainfall; at the end we are buried under the shade of enormous cedars, the same ones that Mackenzie admired. Heart and lungs adjust them- selves to the change of altitude. We are now in the valley of the Bella Coola River, enclosed by precipitous heights, hung with forests and gradually opening, in the course of a thirty- mile route down to the townsite, until the narrow inlet and its terminal tide-flats come into view. A third of the way down this thirty-mile stretch of good road, the point is reached where Mackenzie entered the valley, coming down the northern rim of precipitous cliffs, height above height.

On the return journey he went up the same way and the sight of these walls of rock where snow lingers in August brings back vividly the events of 26 July, 1793. After sleeping under a tree with arms beside him, in case of attack, he had set out at daybreak and by eight o'clock reached Friendly Village. Leaving at eleven, the party had forded a river, Mackenzie carrying the sick Indian, with difficulty, through a rapid waist-deep current. There followed over four hours of precipitous ascent, at the end of which they were too exhausted to gather wood but crawled to fallen pieces and dragged them together for a fire.

Mackenzie's presence is powerfully felt in Bella Coola because the natural setting is still overpowering. No highway or railway has overcome these obstacles and the trip by boat to Vancouver or Victoria is long and expensive. A high proportion of the population is still Indian. Fishing, small-scale lumbering and a little farming have done nothing to change the scene significantly. Nothing crucial has happened since Mackenzie left. It seems natural that he should still be here.

It is the same at the site of Fort Forks, near the junction of the Smoky and Peace Rivers. The valley of the Peace is wide and its contours easy, like the course of prairie rivers, unconfined by rock. A wide and smooth stream. One sees why it was relatively easy, after leaving Athabasca, to come this far and spend the winter here. Trees are plentiful in the wide, hollow valley. In summer there is an abundance of wild roses and nothing to be heard but the buzzing of wasps. Huge banks of sand and gravel show by their long contours the varying force of the current and from round the bend Mackenzie's canoe could appear without surprising anyone.

There are many such reminiscent places. Pine Pass, where the Peace cuts through the actual range of the Rockies, has an altitude of less than three thousand feet. Wooded islands break the broad stream. The Rockies themselves seem here, if here only, to accommodate the river. Why the voyageurs were inseparable from their waterways becomes very clear. It is easy, however, to think of Mackenzie in visual rather than tactile terms. The rushing flood of green water, a background to the varied greens of deciduous and coniferous foliage—he was in the midst of it. The backward curl of waves in the rapids, the gracefully veering, contoured gravel and sand, the shift of the main current from one bank to the other: for Mackenzie these were immediate hazards or helps, to be met with quick and strenuous action. He was wet a great deal of the time. A *décharge*, followed by a steep portage and re-embarkment, was full of bodily hazard, strain and discomfort. Even in Pine Pass, a piece of pure scenic splendour on a summer evening, we are reminded that Mackenzie followed, not the highway but the *fil d'eau*.

It is perhaps at Great Slave Lake that Mackenzie's world opens around one to produce the fullest shock of recognition. Three hundred and fifty miles of gravel road, totally destructive to tyres and windshield, connect Great Slave to the Alberta highway system. There is a port, with fishboats, tugs, barges, wharves and trucks. To the north, across the lake, uranium is mined; to the south, there is drilling for oil. But all of this seems irrelevant to the landscape and the eleven thousand square miles of alternate water and ice. In midsummer the edges of the lake are warm enough for swimming; the mean daily temperature in January is fifteen degrees below zero. The world of affairs, communications and news is very remote and the real centre of things seems here in this nexus of land, water and spreading sky. Innumerable filiations must be extended toward the rest of Canada before this country becomes part of our life. It was Hearne,

Pond and Mackenzie who drew the first threads of communication across its extent.

On this beach, where Mackenzie as *genius loci* visibly lingers, we bid him farewell, watching him withdraw into earth and air and water, here present in all their immensity.

Bibliography

AN edition of the *Voyages*, together with Mackenzie's letters, likely to be definitive, is in preparation by W. Kaye Lamb, the Dominion Archivist, for publication by the Hakluyt Society.

ANDERSON, BERN. *Surveyor of the Sea: The Life and Voyages of Captain George Vancouver*. University of Washington Press, 1960

BISHOP, RICHARD P. *Mackenzie's Rock*, Government Printing Bureau, Ottawa [1924]

BLADEN, V. W. (ed.) *Canadian Population and Northern Colonization: Symposium Presented to the Royal Society of Canada in 1961*, University of Toronto Press, 1962

CAMPBELL, VICE-ADMIRAL GORDON. *Captain James Cook*, Hodder and Stoughton, London, 1936

CAMPBELL, MARJORIE W. *McGillivray: Lord of the Northwest*, Clarke, Irwin and Co., Toronto, 1962

CHITTENDEN, H. M. *The American Fur Trade of the Far West*. Press of the Pioneers, New York, 1935

DAVIDSON, G. C. *The North West Company*, University of California Press, 1918

FRANKLIN, SIR JOHN. *Narrative of a Journey to the Shores of the Polar Sea*, 3rd ed., 2 vols., London, J. Murray, 1824

GATES, CHARLES M. (ed.) *Five Fur Traders of the Northwest*, Minnesota Historical Society, St Paul, 1965. (Five carefully edited and annotated personal accounts, including the narrative of Peter Pond)

GLAZEBROOK, G. P. DE T. *A History of Transportation in Canada: Volume I: Continental Strategy to 1867*. Ryerson Press, Toronto, 1938; reprinted, McClelland and Stewart, Toronto, 1964

GRAY, JOHN M. *Lord Selkirk of Red River*. Macmillan Co. of Canada, Toronto, 1963. (A full and sympathetic account, which incidentally throws much light on the North West Company and its partners)

HEALY, W. J. *Women of Red River*. Women's Canadian Club, Winnipeg, 1923

HEARNE, SAMUEL. *A Journey from Prince of Wales's Fort in Hudson's Bay to the Northern Ocean 1769. 1770. 1771. 1772*, edited by Richard Glover, Macmillan Co. of Canada, Toronto, 1958

HENRY, ALEXANDER. *The Manuscript Journals of Alexander Henry and of David Thompson, 1799–1814*, edited with copious critical commentary by Elliott Coues, 3 vols., Francis P. Harper, New York, 1897. (Although it does not give a transcript of Thompson's journal but rather a digest in a series of footnotes, this work abounds with little-known facts about the fur trade)

HOPWOOD, VICTOR. *David Thompson's Life*, MS (unpublished)

INNIS, HAROLD A. *The Fur Trade in Canada*, Yale University Press, 1930; revised edition, University of Toronto Press, 1956. (A pioneer work of economic analysis, still indispensable)

'Peter Pond, and the Influence of Capt. James Cook on Exploration in the Interior of North America', *Transactions of the Royal Society of Canada*, Third Series, volume XXII, section 2 (1928), pp. 131–41

Peter Pond: Fur Trader and Adventurer, Irwin and Gordon, Toronto, 1930

LANDMANN, GEO. THOMAS. *Adventures and Recollections*, Colburn and Co., London, 1852

MACGREGOR, J. G. *Peter Fidler: Canada's Forgotten Surveyor 1769–1822*, McClelland and Stewart, Toronto, 1966

MACKENZIE, ALEXANDER. *Exploring the Northwest Territory: Sir Alexander Mackenzie's Journal of a Voyage by Bark Canoe from Lake Athabasca to the* [Arctic, not as printer's error has it] *Pacific Ocean in the Summer of 1789*, edited by T. H. McDonald, University of Oklahoma Press, 1966. (Useful notes, many arising from the author's experience in following Mackenzie's route)

First Man West: Alexander Mackenzie's Journal of his Voyage to the Pacific Coast of Canada in 1793, edited by Walter Sheppe, University of California Press, 1962. (Useful notes and appendices, often based on first-hand knowledge)

Journal of a Voyage . . . 1789 #69 University Microfilms, Ann Arbour, Michigan (Stowe MS 793, British Museum Photographic Service)

Voyages from Montreal, on the River St Laurence, through the Continent of North America, to the Frozen and Pacific Oceans; in the Years 1789 and 1793 with a Preliminary Account of the Rise, Progress, and Present State of the Fur Trade of that Country. T. Cadell and W. Davies, London, 1801

NUTE, GRACE L. *The Voyageur,* Appleton, New York, 1931; reprinted Minnesota Historical Society, St Paul, 1955

O'MEARA, WALTER. *The Savage Country,* Houghton Mifflin, Boston, 1960

PLASKETT, J. S. 'The Astronomy of the Explorers', *British Columbia Historical Quarterly,* vol. IV, #2 (April, 1940), pp. 63–77

RICH, E. E. *Montreal and the Fur Trade,* McGill University Press, 1966

ROSS, ALEXANDER. *The Fur Hunters of the Far West,* 2 vols., London, Smith, Elder and Co., 1855

The Fur Hunters of the Far West, edited by K. A. Spaulding, University of Oklahoma Press, 1956

The Red River Settlement, Smith, Elder and Co., London, 1856; reprinted Ross and Haines, Minneapolis, 1957

SELKIRK, [Thomas Douglas, Fifth] Earl of. *A Sketch of the British Fur Trade in North America; with Observations relative to the North-West Company of Montreal,* James Ridgway, London, 1816

SPRY, IRENE M. *The Palliser Expedition: An Account of John Palliser's British North American Expedition 1857–1860,* Macmillan Co. of Canada, Toronto, 1963

STAGER, J. K. 'Alexander Mackenzie's Exploration of the Grand River', *Geographical Bulletin,* vol. VII, nos. 3 & 4 (1965), pp. 213–41. (Most useful: the author has himself followed Mackenzie's course to the Arctic and reconstructs the explorer's daily progress with the aid of large-scale maps)

STEFANSSON, VILHJALMUR. *Not by Bread Alone,* Macmillan, New York, 1946

SWANNELL, F. C. 'Alexander Mackenzie as Surveyor', *The Beaver,* #290 (Winter 1959), pp. 21–5

TAYLOR (?), JAMES. *Pamphlet Ordered to be Printed by the Veterans of the Fur Trade Association Showing Their Ownership of 7,455,552 Acres of Land being the One-Tenth of Lord Selkirk's Estate in the Country Formerly Known as the District of Assiniboia,* Prince Albert, 1906

THOMPSON, DAVID. *Journals,* Microfilm R1511: 1–6, Library of the University of British Columbia

Narrative 1784–1812, edited by Richard Glover, Champlain Society, Toronto, 1962

BIBLIOGRAPHY

VAIL, PHILIP. *The Magnificent Adventures of Alexander Mackenzie*, Dodd, Mead & Co., New York, 1964. (This account includes a voyageur for whom I have not as yet been able to find the source)

WADE, M. S. *Mackenzie of Canada: The Life and Adventures of Alexander Mackenzie, Discoverer*, Blackwood, Edinburgh, 1927. (A well-rounded account, with much historical background. A labour of love)

WAGNER, HENRY R. *Peter Pond: Fur Trader and Explorer*, Yale University Library, 1955. (A set of indispensable maps accompanies the text)

WARKENTIN, JOHN (ed.) *The Western Interior of Canada. A Record of Geographical Discovery 1612–1917*, McClelland and Stewart, Toronto, 1964

[WILCOCKE, S. H.] *A Narrative of Occurrences in the Indian Countries of North America, since the Connexion of the Right Hon. the Earl of Selkirk with the Hudson's Bay Company, and his Attempt to Establish a Colony on the Red River; with a Detailed Account of His Lordship's Military Expedition to, and Subsequent Proceedings at Fort William, in Upper Canada*, Nahum Mower, London, 1817, reprinted Montreal, 1818

WOOLLACOTT, A. P. *Mackenzie and his Voyageurs*, Dent, London, 1927

WRONG, HUME. *Sir Alexander Mackenzie: Explorer and Fur-Trader*, Macmillan, Toronto, 1927

Index

Johnson, John, 165
Jolliet, Louis, 54, 200
Juan de Fuca, Strait of, 195

Kamchatka (Kampschatka, Kam
    skatsha), 36, 46
Kelsey, Henry, 199
Kenneth (chief), 46
Kensington Palace, 183
Kent, Duke of, 165, 170, 183
Kildonan (Red River), 180; (Scot-
    land), 180
Killicrankie, Pass of, 186
King George's Sound, 172
King's Royal Regiment, 51
Kingston, 167
Kintail, 46, 47
Kirkcudbrightshire, 178
Knisteneaux Indians, *see* Cree
Kootenae (Kootenay) House, 194
Kwakiutl Indians, 149

La Chine (Lachine), 29, 166
Landmann, George Thomas, 22,
    165, 166, 167, 169
Landry, Joseph, 61, 111
La Salle, Robert de, 200
Lawrence, Thomas, 33
Lena River, 46
Le Roux (Leroux) (trader), 30,
    61, 63, 64, 68, 69, 86, 87
Lesseps, Ferdinand de, 93
Lewis, 47, 49
Lewis, Meriwether, 176, 194, 196
Liard River, 18, 72
Loche, Lac la, 161
London, 14, 24, 30, 36, 40, 45,
    164, 173, 176, 181, 182, 183, 184,
    187, 189
Long Island, 47
Lorme, Pierre de, 61
Louisiana, 195
Lower Canada, 163, 176

Loyalists, 50

McArthur (army officer), 166
MacDonald, John A., 96
    (clerk), 103
    T. H., 86, 97
Macdonnell, Miles, 179, 180
McGillivray, Duncan, 165
    Simon, 179
    William, 52, 166, 167, 179
McGregor River, 130, 158
Maciver family, 47
Mackay, Alexander, 92, 111, 114,
    115, 120, 121, 122, 129, 133,
    137, 138, 140, 142, 149, 152,
    153, 154, 159
Mackenzie, Alexander (junior),
    184, 187
    Andrew, 182
    Donald, 185
    Geddes, 182, 186
    George, 184, 187
    Kenneth, 47
    Margaret, 47
    Margaret Geddes, 184, 187
    Murdoch, 47, 48
Mackenzie River, 14, 18, 59, 82,
    94, 189, 202
Mackenzie, Roderick and family,
    30, 43, 51, 52, 53, 90, 97, 98,
    103, 161, 176, 184, 185, 186,
    202
    Sybilla, 47
McLeod, Archibald (?), 89
    Normand, 51
McTavish, Simon, 164, 165, 169,
    175, 189, 198, 203
Macubah, *see* Vancouver
Manchester, 28
Manitoba, 27, 52
Marlborough, John Churchill, 1st
    Duke of, 19
Marquette, Jacques, 54, 200